ISAAC BASHEVIS SINGER

ISAAC BASHEVIS SINGER

An Album

Edited by Ilan Stavans

*Biographical commentary
by James Gibbons*

THE LIBRARY OF AMERICA

See page 126 for photo copyrights and acknowledgments.

"Greenhorn in Sea Gate" © 1985 by Isaac Bashevis Singer.
Published by special arrangement with Lescher & Lescher, Ltd.
All rights reserved.

The paper used in this publication meets the
minimum requirements of the American National Standard for
Information Sciences—Permanence of Paper for Printed
Library Materials, ANSI z39.48—1984.

Distributed to the trade in the United States
by Penguin Putnam, Inc.
and in Canada by Penguin Books Canada Ltd.

Library of Congress Cataloging-in-Publication Data
Isaac Bashevis Singer: an album / edited by Ilan
Stavans.
p.   cm.
ISBN 1-931082-64-2
1. Singer, Isaac Bashevis, 1904–1991 2. Singer, Isaac
Bashevis, 1904–1991—Anecdotes. 3. Authors,
Yiddish—Biography. I. Stavans, Ilan.
PJ5129.S49Z4628 2004
839'.133—dc22   2004044105

10 9 8 7 6 5 4 3 2 1

Printed in the United States of America

Contents

Appreciations

I. Sketch of Singer by Laura Ziegler, 1971.

Preface

Isaac Bashevis Singer and The Library of America

W HAT MAKES a writer an American writer? The accident of his birth or perhaps the circumstances of his exile? His language? His themes? Where he is published? His audience?

The works of Isaac Bashevis Singer, the seventh American citizen to be awarded the Nobel Prize for literature, and whose centennial is celebrated in 2004, raise these questions in particularly fascinating ways. He was born in Poland and wrote virtually all his work in Yiddish, even after he immigrated to the United States in 1935 at age 30—yet he lived in New York City for more than 50 years and set many of his stories there. His writing drew on East European Jewish folk memory and mystical traditions, and on a *shtetl* culture that was worlds away from the glare and the blare of postwar America. Yet the fictional world he created spoke movingly to the fears, longings, and ambivalence about assimilation of modern Americans, and Singer found himself lionized by the literary establishment, published in such magazines as *Partisan Review*, *Harper's*, *The New Yorker,* and *Playboy*, and by the distinguished firm of Farrar, Straus & Giroux. In his apartment on Manhattan's Upper West Side, Singer conjured parables of Old World demons and holy fools. And his parables seemed, to his newfound American audience, startlingly apposite to the morally ambiguous world ushered in by World War II, even as they evoked, as in a dream, a time and a place that the war had brutally obliterated.

This special publication of The Library of America is part of *Becoming an American Writer*, a national centennial celebration exploring Singer's life and work. It is a reader's companion in a double sense: to the publication in The Library of America series of Singer's collected stories in an authoritative three-volume edition, and to a traveling exhibition, curated by the Harry Ransom Humanities Research Center at the University of Texas, from whose collections many of the following images are drawn. The Singer Centennial is supported by a generous grant from the National Endowment for the Humanities.

But *Singer: An Album* is more than a companion—it is also the most reliable guide available to a multifaceted life, a life that remains surprisingly unfamiliar despite Singer's memoirs. Like many writers, he could be an unreliable guide to his own biography, selectively raiding his memories for his own literary purposes. This volume attempts to tell what is known, to help the reader put Singer's imaginative work in an accurate and carefully documented context. To grasp the facts of Singer's years in Warsaw and Bilgoray, in Brooklyn and Manhattan and Miami Beach, is to add even more layers to the experience of reading him, an experience that involves, as Alfred Kazin wrote, "moving through as many historical levels as an archaeologist at work."

One crucial part of Singer's "becoming an American writer" was the translation of his work from Yiddish into English, an undertaking in which he participated as full partner with his translators. Translation inevitably involves change, which is to say both loss and gain, as a literary work finds a new home as part of a different cultural tradition. With Singer's publication in The Library of America, in an edition edited by Ilan Stavans, new connections are established, new affinities discovered between his work and that of other American writers in the series—Hawthorne and Melville most obviously, but also Irving and Poe, Faulkner, Nathanael West, and Saul Bellow.

Like many of his contemporaries, Singer had qualms about the direction, the relentless commercialism, of postwar American society, and he emphasized that the literary tradition from which he emerged was stateless. Nevertheless, he was unambivalent about his own American translation, both physical and literary. "If you ask me from an *emotional* point of view," he once said, "I don't feel myself a foreigner because I love America and I love the American people. And since my own country, Poland, where I was born, almost does not exist as far as I am concerned—it's a different world there—the U.S. is my real home now. So just as English has become to me a second original, America is to me my real country."

In that spirit, we welcome Isaac Bashevis Singer into The Library of America and, with gratitude and admiration for his enormous imaginative gifts, wish him happy birthday.

Max Rudin
Publisher, The Library of America
Director, Isaac Bashevis Singer Centennial

April 2004

Beginnings

ALTHOUGH ISAAC SINGER spent much of his childhood in Warsaw, his roots were in the Jewish folk culture of the villages and market towns scattered throughout the Lublin region of eastern Poland. In these communities, traditional forms of Jewish life persisted well into the twentieth century. In his book of sketches about his childhood, *In My Father's Court*, Singer remembers fleeing Warsaw with his mother and brother Moishe during World War I to settle in Bilgoray, where his grandfather had served for some forty years as the town's rabbi. "My grandfather had insulated Bilgoray against evil temptation, and the town's distance from the railroad helped," Singer recalled. "The Yiddish I heard there and the kind of Jewish behavior and customs I witnessed were those preserved from a much earlier time." If he hadn't lived in Bilgoray, Singer once told an interviewer, he would not have been able to write his first book, *Satan in Goray*, a novel set in the seventeenth century, or many of his short stories. "In this world of old Jewishness I found a spiritual treasure trove," he wrote in *In My Father's Court*. "I had a chance to see our past as it really was. Time seemed to flow backwards. I lived Jewish history."

Singer's sense of life in a Jewish village provided a seemingly inexhaustible source for his stories, novels, and memoirs. But his feelings about village life and culture were complex, often critical, sometimes contradictory. In parts of *In My Father's Court,* his idealized and nostalgic sense of Bilgoray as a repository of Jewish tradition and history was a view shaped by the trauma of the Holocaust and the annihilation of Jewish culture in Poland. Elsewhere in his autobiographical writings he recalls being unhappy in Bilgoray, where his family was dependent on charity and pious members of the community frowned upon his attempts to write poems and stories rather than study the Talmud. "In the wintertime Bilgoray seemed like a drab Siberian village, fit only for exiled prisoners," he wrote in the memoir "From the Old and New Home," serialized in the *Jewish Daily Forward* from 1963 to 1965. "We were refugees, and we were treated like refugees."

By the time Singer left Warsaw in 1917, the Jewish village was no longer insulated from the modern world. Bilgoray itself was occupied by Austrian troops. The railroad that had been far enough away to pose no threat of distracting villagers from the admonitions of Singer's grandfather had reached the town at last. The secular ideas of the *Haskalah*, or Jewish Enlightenment, were debated, defended,

2. Woodcut by Antonio Frasconi, from an illustrated edition (1983) of "Yentl the Yeshiva Boy."

and reviled even in the smallest villages. "Processes that elsewhere had developed over decades materialized here literally overnight," Singer wrote in 1943. "Young yeshiva students who had not yet shed their slitted gaberdines and little caps, and who were still up to their necks in the legacy of generations, suddenly decided that waiting for the Messiah was not for them; that the shops in which their fathers stood were a contemptible and unreliable source of livelihood; that it was altogether unpleasant to have gentile rowdies throw stones and shout 'Jew' after you; that in the little shtetlekh [village] one lived in filth, in ignorance, and that something had to be done to extricate oneself from the mire. . . . Here in Poland, entire houses of study were emptied overnight. The Zionist, socialist, and communist movements snatched most of the young people. Organizations, clubs, and libraries sprouted like mushrooms after a rain."

3. Jewish cemetery in Frampol, 1985. Singer's story "The Gentleman from Cracow" begins with a description of the village: "Amid thick forests and deep swamps, on the slope of a hill, level at the summit, lay the village of Frampol. Nobody knew who had founded it, or why just there. Goats grazed among the tombstones which were already sunk in the ground of the cemetery."

4. Singer's maternal grandfather, the rabbi of Bilgoray. "He was the kind of Rabbi who lived in the past," Singer wrote. "To the few sophisticates in Bilgoray, Grandfather was a fanatic, a purveyor of darkness, but despite this, he was respected and feared. . . . His command was like that of the ancient leaders, and while he lived, Bilgoray remained pious."

Krochmalna Street
1908–1917

IN 1908, the Singer family moved to Warsaw, where Singer's father presided over a rabbinical court that served local residents as a "blend of a court of law, synagogue, house of study, and, if you will, psychoanalyst's office where people of troubled spirit could come to unburden themselves." With its theaters, newspapers, Zionist and Bundist meetings, kiosks selling melodramatic novels, and petty crime, Warsaw offered a life far different than that of Leoncin, the dusty hamlet where Singer was born, or Radzymin, the town where his father had briefly in 1904 directed the local yeshiva. While life in these villages bore the stamp of the past, the twentieth century was well underway in Warsaw's Jewish quarter when the family arrived in the city. Singer recalled crowds gaping at their first glimpses of the automobile, and memories of the 1905 anti-czarist uprising were fresh in the minds of the quarter's inhabitants. His mother found the city a Gehenna of iniquity; his father, scandalized by girls dressed in the latest fashions, warned against "salacious females who uncovered their flesh to arouse men to evil thoughts," and made sure that his family avoided eating cakes baked in Warsaw on Purim because "we were never certain how conscientious Warsaw Jews were about the dietary regulations."

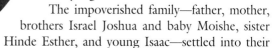

5. Singer in 1926, at the age of 22.

The impoverished family—father, mother, brothers Israel Joshua and baby Moishe, sister Hinde Esther, and young Isaac—settled into their second-floor apartment at 10 Krochmalna Street, living in three sparsely furnished rooms, the walls bare so as not to encourage the idolatrous habit of gazing upon a graven image. Viewed from the balcony that looked out on the street, a perch where Hinde Esther would spend hours watching passersby, the world outside was bustling, clamorous, awash in a riot of sounds and smells. The neighborhood had a seedy side as well, as streetwalkers and pickpockets mingled with pious Jews on Krochmalna Street and shopkeepers paid protection money to

6. Krochmalna Street, Warsaw.

7. Asher the dairyman, the subject of one of the sketches collected in *In My Father's Court.* "There are some people in this world who are simply born good. Such was Reb Asher the dairyman. God had endowed him with many, many gifts."

8. Roman Vishniac. *Selling Geese*, ca. 1938. Gelatin silver print. This photo was included in *A Day of Pleasure*, an adaptation of Singer's autobiographical writings for children. In "Why the Geese Shrieked" in *In My Father's Court*, the shrieking of dead geese illustrates Singer's parents' divergent attitudes toward inexplicable phenomena: his father looks for answers in his holy books, whereas his "rationalist" mother puts a halt to the noises by ripping out the geese's windpipes.

gang leaders like Blind Itche, who later made an appearance as one of the more brutal characters in Singer's novel *Yarme and Keyle*.

While living on Krochmalna Street, Singer attended a series of *cheder*s (religious primary schools) and received a Jewish education that was supplemented by lessons from his parents. Despite his father's disapproval, he began to read secular literature, enjoying detective stories and browsing with fascination through his brother's copy of *Crime and Punishment*. At home Singer heard fierce arguments between his parents and the older children Israel Joshua and Hinde Esther, both of whom resisted familial expectations. Determined to lead a secular life, Israel Joshua moved out of the house at the age of eighteen. Hinde Esther, a "Hasid in skirts" who suffered from "mild attacks of epilepsy" and at times "seemed possessed by a dibbuk," consented to an arranged marriage with diamond cutter Abraham Kreitman and moved to Antwerp in 1912. Like their younger brother Isaac, both Israel Joshua and Hinde Esther became novelists.

In 1914, the family moved to a larger apartment next door at 12 Krochmalna Street. When German troops occupied Warsaw the following year, many Polish Jews welcomed the end of Russian rule in the city. They were quickly disabused of their illusions. Novelist Zalman Shneour wrote of the occupation that the Jews were "struck by a permanent German pogrom, which blighted them body and soul like a disease, and from which there was no escape." A typhus epidemic worsened an already dire situation; Krochmalna Street was hit especially hard, and after Singer's brother Moishe fell ill with the disease Singer and his mother were quarantined for more than a week. "Mother and I were taken to the disinfecting station on Szczesliwa Street near the Jewish cemetery," he recalled in his autobiographical novel *Shosha*. "There they shaved off my earlocks and fed me soup flavored with pork. For me—the son of a rabbi—these were spiritual calamities." In the summer of 1917, Singer and his mother left Warsaw for Bilgoray.

9. Singer's sister, Hinde Esther (Kreitman), June 1935. The following year she published the novel, *Der sheydim-tants* (*The Devil's Dance*, later translated into English by her son Maurice Carr as *Deborah*).

10. Roman Vishniac. *On the Way to His First Day at Chedar, Mukachevo*, 1938, gelatin silver print, also included in *A Day of Pleasure*.

A Young Writer in Warsaw
1921–1935

RETURNING TO Warsaw in 1921, Singer entered the Tachkemoni Rabbinical Seminary and spent a difficult year as a poor, dispirited, and often hungry student. The two years that followed were an aimless, unhappy period: abandoning his studies at the seminary, Singer went back to Bilgoray, accepted a position teaching in a nearby town (an experience recounted in the story "A Tutor in the Village"), then lived for nine months in Dzikow, the "half-bog, half-village" where his father was serving as rabbi. By now he had read many of the books, sacred and profane, that would exert such a strong influence on his imagination: the novels of Tolstoy and Knut Hamsun, the Kabbalah, Spinoza's *Ethics*. Describing his time in Dzikow, Singer later wrote that he was so broken in spirit that he was ready to give in to his parents, accept an arranged marriage, and make a humble life for himself as a village shopkeeper or teacher. The breadth of his curiosity and his voracious reading—which encompassed not just literature and philosophy but popular science and the occult—suggests that he exaggerated his sense of resignation. As a young man stranded in the provinces, Singer felt keenly the lure of Warsaw's cosmopolitan atmosphere, its intellectual ferment, thriving literary scene, and not least its relaxed attitudes toward sex. When Israel Joshua secured him a job as a proofreader in 1923, Singer moved back to the city, now the capital of the recently founded Polish republic, and spent the next decade establishing himself as a writer.

11. Israel Joshua Singer in his twenties.

Israel Joshua was already a rising literary star. He had returned to Poland after living in Kiev and Moscow, where he worked for Yiddish newspapers, wrote plays, and witnessed the Bolshevik Revolution firsthand. "Here I saw Jewish blood flow—rivers of blood," he recalled in 1927. "Here I glimpsed life, real life, that ruined all theories and illusions about people and nations." In Warsaw he affiliated himself briefly with the avant-garde group "Di khaliastre" ("The Gang"), published the story collection *Pearls*, and co-founded the journal *Literarishe bleter*

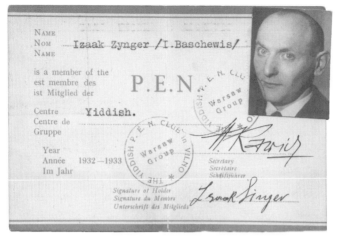

12. Yiddish P.E.N. Club identification card, 1932–1933. International P.E.N. was founded in 1921 with the liberal aims of promoting cooperation among writers and opposing censorship. The first P.E.N. Club was established in London by C. A. Dawson Scott and John Galsworthy; the Yiddish P.E.N. Club, accredited in 1926, was the first branch of the organization dedicated to a minority literature within a nation.

13. Singer (*rear center*) with other Yiddish writers in Warsaw during the 1930s. *Left to right*: K. Molodovsky, Y. Kirman, Y. Opatoshu, A. Zeitlin, M. Ravitch.

(*Literary Pages*). In the United States, the novelist and editor Abraham Cahan, impressed with his abilities as a fiction writer, invited him to contribute regularly to the *Jewish Daily Forward* in New York. Suddenly Israel Joshua had a readership on two continents. His prominence in Yiddish letters ensured that his younger brother was introduced to writers like Peretz Markish and Melekh Ravitch, the poet who provided free lodging in his attic apartment when Singer arrived in Warsaw. Israel Joshua's success was a blessing, but a decidedly mixed one, providing a model for Singer to emulate but also burdening the brothers' relationship with the tensions of literary rivalry.

The most important institution for Yiddish writers in Poland in the 1920s was the Association of Jewish Writers and Journalists, with headquarters in Warsaw at 13 Tlomackie Street, next door to the city's largest synagogue. Singer was often seen at this "bourse of Yiddish literature in Poland," where writers took meals together, played chess, attended lectures, debated philosophy and current events, squabbled over literary politics, and struck up romantic liaisons. Attracting would-be poets and novelists from all over Poland, the Yiddish P.E.N. Club (as the association was called after its accreditation by P.E.N. in 1926) was not without its eccentrics, cranks, pedants, and misfit prodigies:

> New arrivals to the Writers' Union included a regimental colonel and government rabbi whose ritual fringes stuck out from under his uniform; a young man who had written an encyclopedia on his own and who had entire sacks filled with manuscripts; a poor woman who wrote refined pornographic poems; and a man who took out an ad in the papers on the eve of every festival, claiming that the coming of the Messiah had been revealed to him. There were Hebrew teachers who spent hours arguing over points of grammar; a Bundist who had once had to eliminate a stool pigeon and who never stopped conducting conspiracies; a Jew who bathed in winter, ate only vegetables, and believed in Jesus; and a librarian familiar with every cranny of world literature who nonetheless could not believe—did not want to believe—that there was such a thing as a literature in Yiddish.

Such outrageous types notwithstanding, the P.E.N. Club nurtured the most talented Yiddish writers in Poland. Guest lecturers visiting from the United States, Palestine, and elsewhere in Europe facilitated exchange among Yiddish writers worldwide. Enduring bonds were forged among the P.E.N. Club's members and often bore fruit in the form of collaborative anthologies and magazines. A case in point is Singer's long association with the poet Aaron Zeitlin. In 1932, eight years after meeting at 13 Tlomackie Street, they founded the magazine *Globus*, which published several of Singer's stories and serialized his first novel, *Der sotn in Goray* (*Satan in Goray*).

Singer's first published story, a grim naturalistic tale entitled "Oyf der elter" ("In Old Age"), appeared in *Literarishe bleter* in 1925 and won first prize in a competition sponsored by the journal. It was an auspicious debut for Singer, still finding his way as a writer and not even certain whether to continue writing in Yiddish. Flirting with the idea of switching to Hebrew as his literary language, he published two stories in the Hebrew newspaper *Ha-yom* (*Today*) and signed them "Yitskhok Bashevis," a pseudonym adapted from Basheve, his mother's name. He soon resumed writing in Yiddish but kept the pseudonym, using it to sign most of his Yiddish fiction for the rest of his career. His stories and reviews began appearing regularly in *Literarishe bleter* and other publications, but Singer could barely scrape together a living. To help support himself he wrote potboilers for the newspaper *Radio* and translated several novels into Yiddish,

14. Aaron Zeitlin

including Knut Hamsun's *Pan*, Thomas Mann's *The Magic Mountain*, and Erich Maria Remarque's *All Quiet on the Western Front*. In the 1930s he also contributed articles to the Paris Yiddish newspaper *Parizer Haynt* (*Paris Daily*).

By far the most substantial achievement of Singer's Warsaw years, and perhaps his entire career, was his first novel, *Satan in Goray*. Set in the middle of the seventeenth century, the novel takes place in the tiny village of Goray, a "town that lay in the midst of hills at the end of the world," an isolated enclave whose diminutive size and insularity is meant to suggest an archetypal Eastern European Jewish community. Despite its remoteness, Goray is swept up in the cataclysms of history. The novel opens with a description of the near-destruction of the village in 1648, as part of the genocidal wave of violence against the Jews instigated by Cossack leader Bohdan Chmielnicki: "They slaughtered on every hand, flayed men alive, murdered small children, violated women and afterward ripped open their bellies and sewed cats inside. Many fled to Lublin, many underwent baptism or were sold into slavery." Most of *Satan in Goray* unfolds seventeen years later, by which time the village had returned to a semblance of the life it had known before the carnage. But a restoration of former harmony and prosperity, of a time in which "living was easy, and Jewishness in high repute," is impossible. Reb Eleazer Babad, once a revered and wealthy merchant, has become an unrecognizable husk of his former self, his body stooped, his clothes no better than a beggar's, his mind unhinged by despair. His daughter Rechele, a mere infant in 1648, endures a harrowing childhood in the wake of the massacres and grows up to be a disturbed young woman "beset by mysterious ills," given to impious outbursts and fits of emotion. And the town's rabbi, though "reckoned among the most brilliant men of the day," is too old to summon the strength necessary to make peace among warring parties, even those of his own family.

15. Cover of *Oyfn hayrev-front keyn nayes* (1930), Singer's Yiddish translation of Erich Maria Remarque's *All Quiet on the Western Front* (1929).

Into this troubled village, marked by communal disarray and malaise, come emissaries of Sabbatai Zevi, the kabbalist from Smyrna who had attracted a mass following after declaring himself the messiah in 1648, the fateful year of Chmielnicki's depredations. A ferocious dispute about whether Sabbatai Zevi is in fact the messiah convulses the community of Goray, unleashing violence in the study house and rousing ecstatic hopes of the coming redemption among the town's Sabbatean converts. Orgiastic rites replace traditional observance. The village is transformed beyond recognition. The strife in miniscule Goray takes on cosmic significance as Satan himself joins the battle, preying on Rechele and impregnating her.

This seemingly distant conflict within Judaism plays out as something far more powerful than simply a reconstruction of the seventeenth century—though Singer's vivid imagining of the past, his gift for evoking the sensual world of *shtetl* life, and his adaptation of the world view of ordinary villagers to his own literary ends are among his fundamental strengths as a writer. Envisioning a world of merciless anti-Semitism and a Jewish community shaken to its core by messianic claims of uncertain but quite probably devastating import, Singer immersed himself in the past to comment on the present. As *Satan in Goray*'s translator Jacob Sloan noted in his preface to the American edition: "In this work we see, foreshadowed by three centuries as it were, adumbrations of our own twentieth century attempts at personal transformation through hysterical activism." In remarks

16. Press card for *Parizer Haynt* (*Paris Daily*).

17. Singer with his cousin Esther, walking in Zakopane, a resort town in the Carpathian Mountains. "When Esther spoke I could hear in her words, and even more so in her intonation, generations of scholars, pious women, as well as something that seemed non-Jewish, even typically goyish."

about the book Singer drew parallels between the Sabbatean movement and twentieth-century fascism and totalitarianism. As such *Satan in Goray* is as much a political allegory as a historical novel. Singer's brilliance lies in his decision to address the political and cultural upheaval he observed all around him by *not* writing a topical novel. Drawing on Jewish traditions that many of his contemporaries had dismissed, he imbued *Satan in Goray* with an aura of mythic, metaphysical struggle.

Singer was involved with several women during his Warsaw years—indeed, his not-always-reliable memoir about the period is entitled *A Young Man in Search of Love*. One of his mistresses was Runia Shapira, a rabbi's daughter who had become an ardent communist; their son Israel, Singer's only child, was born in 1929. The couple separated in 1935, when both decided to emigrate but chose different destinations: Runia took Israel to the Soviet Union, and Singer—with the help of Israel Joshua, now working for the *Jewish Daily Forward* in New York—went to America. Leaving Poland, never to return, Singer now entered a new, uncertain phase as he began his long exile in the United States.

18. Runia Shapira and son Israel, c. March 14, 1936. In 1937, Runia was denounced as a Zionist by the Soviet authorities and given 24 hours to leave the country. After spending nine months in Turkey, she settled with her son in Palestine. Although Singer corresponded with Runia sporadically throughout the 1930s and 1940s, he did not see his son Israel (who took the last name "Zamir") until 1955.

19. Framed photo of Singer as a young man.

20. Singer's Hebrew-character typewriter, which he bought shortly after his arrival in New York and used for the rest of his career. "I have a Yiddish typewriter which is very capricious and highly critical," he explained in 1976. "If this typewriter doesn't like a story, it refuses to work."

Greenhorn

My First Steps in the Golden Land

by Isaac Bashevis Singer

This essay, a reminiscence of Singer's first months in America, was published in The New York Times Magazine *on November 3, 1985.*

I ARRIVED in New York in 1935, in the time of the Depression. The older people I met in Sea Gate, Brooklyn, where my brother, the writer I. J. Singer, lived during the summer, all spoke about the fortunes they had amassed in the time of the Prosperity and the great losses they had suffered in the Wall Street Crash.

They all seemed to be has-been millionaires. As a writer in Yiddish, I felt like a has-been myself. Abe Cahan, the editor of *The Jewish Daily Forward*, kept repeating in his editorials that Yiddish had only one mission: to help bring Socialism and then disappear forever. Even the Yiddish journalists and writers I met in the Royal Cafe on Second Avenue contended that my writings had no relevance in America, neither for the Jews nor for the Gentiles.

Who was going to be interested in a false Messiah who lived some 300 years ago? Who would believe in the lore of the cabala, in such superstitions as reincarnation, dybbuks, haunted houses, girls seduced by demons,

21. Two photomat portraits of Isaac Singer, circa 1936.

in Sea Gate

corpses rising from their graves and other such balderdash? The world was moving forward, not backward. I agreed with them. I seemed to have been born an anachronism.

Yet I was actually comfortable in the role of an anachronism. The young women felt sorry for me. Since the Polish quota was filled and I could get only a tourist visa to be renewed every six months, it seemed that I would have

22. Cover and pages from Singer's Polish passport. The date of the last stamp indicates Singer's final departure from Poland on April 17, 1935.

to return to a Poland that was about to be invaded by Hitler. I was for them as good as dead. They drank coffee with me in the cafeteria on Mermaid Avenue. They comforted me and we indulged in casual love affairs. We went to the movies during the day, when the admission was 15 cents, and we took long walks on the boardwalk. Whenever we spoke about the Jews and Jewishness, these girls would say, "In what way am I Jewish? I know nothing about Jews and Jewish culture. I was not even taught the Hebrew alphabet. My parents spoke Yiddish only when they didn't want us to understand what they were saying." Zionism was promoting a sheer utopia, they were saying. England would never give up her mandate over Palestine. And why settle down in an Asiatic country surrounded with millions of hostile Arabs? When the revolution came, it would come there too. After the end of the summer, my brother and his family moved back to Manhattan. I had renewed my visa for another six months. A fatalistic indifference had overcome me. I rented a room in Sea

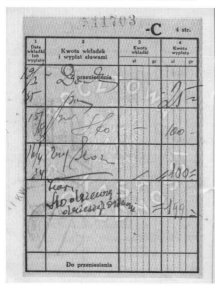

Gate for $4 a week. The cold, the snow and the frost had set in. At night the wind howled, the bell of the lighthouse rang, the ocean stormed and foamed with a rage as old as eternity.

I had nothing to do in the short winter days and the long winter nights, and I turned back in my writing to the demons, the devils, the hobgoblins, the creatures of the night. I had heard about immigrants falling into melancholy after arriving in America, and now I could identify myself with them. Everything seemed unreal to me, as strange as if by some cosmic error my ship had docked on another planet, in a far-off constellation, on a duplicate Mother Earth or its shadow in the universe. I was not myself anymore. The people around me spoke to me, but their words had lost their meaning. I cannot believe it now, but I seriously considered returning to Poland. Quite a few writers and intellectuals did return, some of them as late as August 1939.

I felt then and I feel now that literature has neglected the terrible trauma of those who are

23. While living in Sea Gate, Singer often visited the house of Bella Dykaar, the widow of sculptor Moses Dykaar. Singer and Bella posed for this photograph at Coney Island in the mid-1930s. "She was a beautiful woman, herself a painter who wrote poetry," Singer later recalled. "From morning till night the intellectuals sat on the porch and discussed Jewishness, Zionism, Socialism, English and Russian literature, as well as the works of Hebrew and Yiddish writers."

24. The Singer brothers, from an article in the *Jewish Daily Forward*, June 2, 1935.

forced to leave their land, abandon their language and begin a new life somewhere else. Disruption of this kind must be especially painful to artists—writers and actors whose linguistic roots are the essence of their creation. In my case, not only was I cut off from my language but I also felt my way of thinking, my notions and my concepts, had been distorted. There was no place for demons in the din and clamor of Manhattan or Coney Island. Synagogues in this city resembled churches, boys played football in front of their yeshivas. Mortuaries were built alongside banks, restaurants or garages and the coffins were carried into limousines. As to the mourners, they could just as well have been guests at a wedding.

I could no longer recognize my people by their speech patterns, their dress, their gestures and mannerisms. The women appeared tough to me. They smoked cigarettes and spoke like men. I imagined that something of a mental catastrophe had taken place here, some sort of biological and cultural mutation for which I could find no words in my Yiddish vocabulary. How could I seriously love those smart American women, I asked myself. My old bashfulness, that I had tried so hard to hide in the years I struggled to become a worldly writer, came back to me. I had heard the word "greenhorn" when I was still in Warsaw, and I knew that this is what I was—a perfect misfit. My brother wanted to introduce me to people, to make a party for me, but I refused with a stubbornness that was almost insulting to him and to my sister-in-law.

I am not exaggerating when I say it took me years to get over this crisis. It is actually still with me. However, I have learned in those years that a crisis—any crisis—can become a treasure for a creative person. It might very well be that the great American novel that is often referred to by critics and of which many writers dream will not describe native Americans but immigrants who settle here—their alienation, their utter confusion, their efforts to compensate for their uprooted lives. As my Aunt Yentl used to say, "There is no evil from which something good does not come out."

25, 26. *Left*: A list of English words and their Yiddish translations compiled by Singer. *Above*: A page from his 1940 daily planner, which doubled as an English glossary.

Nicholas Dawidoff:

Ever since I've known my father's mother, my Grandma Rebecca, she has lived in a Greenwich Village apartment not far from New York University. It's a pleasant set of rooms, quiet, sun-filled, and spacious enough to contain a den in which she long ago installed a set of bookshelves. My grandmother finds reading more difficult these days—she is 95—but through most of her life, to look in on her collection of books was to see the world she lived in. There were biographies of American and foreign leaders, exhibition catalogues of modern French painters, novels by contemporary masters from London and Chicago. There was also *Passions*, a collection of stories by Isaac Bashevis Singer. I developed an idea about how *Passions* got there. I decided that somebody sentimental must have given it to her. After all, Fina-Rivka Rosenberg had come to this country from Warsaw as a Yiddish-speaking toddler and grew up in tenement flats on the Lower East Side sharing a bed with her sister Rachel. Eventually she elevated herself; in 1929, she became one of the first women to graduate with a law degree from New York University. By

27. Hester Street, between Allen and Orchard streets, 1938.

the time I met her she was Rebecca Dawidoff Rolland, an assimilated American lawyer—she called her beef brisket "Yankee pot roast"—and a successful secular woman who emanated a pedigree that was, if anything, New Deal, not old neighborhood. As she had once told me, "I wanted to get rid of those days. I wanted to be an American, not let everybody know that I was little Rivka from Varsha." My assumptions about *Passions* were that because the Eastern European Jewish immigrant experience was something she hoped to distance herself from, Singer, a writer documenting that experience, would be similarly tainted. Yet recently she told me that, in fact, when she first began reading Singer's stories in *The New Yorker*, "He brought me back to my old days, the people and the accents and the sounds of my old days that I wanted to get rid of. When I met Singer I was quite surprised to find him talking about that era. I never thought that my early way of life would be anything of interest to anybody in the future who read books. It seemed so amazing. Here was somebody—a recognized author—writing about the life I was living. He was recording me! It certainly made you feel

28. Storefront at 55 Hester Street on New York's Lower East Side, 1937.

more worthy." As she said this, it occurred to me that a woman's ambivalence about shedding her ethnic past was the sort of quintessentially American subject that resonates in the stories of Singer, a writer who has been marginalized on some people's bookshelves because he wrote in a so-called Jewish idiom. How my grandmother came to view that sort of thinking was clear when she cast her eye back over her life with Singer and said, "I finally decided that the fact that a writer was interested in my background was a very American sort of thing."

Struggling with America
1935–1942

THE FIRST novel Singer wrote in America, *Der zindiker meshiekh* (*The Sinning Messiah*), was published in serialized installments in the *Jewish Daily Forward* and in Yiddish newspapers in Warsaw and Paris. Like *Satan in Goray*, it was a historical novel about false messianism, in this case a treatment of the life of eighteenth-century Jewish heretic Jacob Frank, who claimed to be Sabbatai Zevi reincarnated. Singer considered *The Sinning Messiah* a failure and never attempted to publish it as a book. In *Lost in America*, a memoir about his early years in New York, he describes his experience writing the novel as unusually strained and painful, fraught with fears of imminent humiliation and exposure as a literary fraud. These anxieties were at least partly bound up with Singer's peculiar position as the brother of a novelist whose work was now read and acclaimed in America well beyond his primary Yiddish audience. In 1936, shortly after *The Sinning Messiah* was completed, Israel Joshua published his epic novel *Di brider Ashkenazi (The Brothers Ashkenazi)* in Yiddish and in an English translation that was praised by critics and soon became a best seller. For Isaac, the stature of his older brother helped secure the publication of his work in the *Forward* and brought him instant notoriety among its readers as yet another novelist in this family of writers. "Nearly everyone used the same cliché—that I had gotten off 'on the right foot in America' while other writers had had

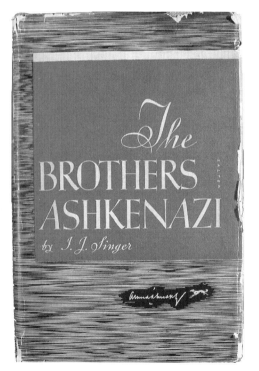

29. Dust jacket of first edition of I. J. Singer's *The Brothers Ashkenazi*, translated by Maurice Samuel and published by Knopf in 1936, from the Isaac Bashevis Singer collection at the Harry Ransom Center, University of Texas at Austin. The novel was soon translated into several other languages.

to wait years to get their names in the paper." Inevitably, there was grumbling, which Singer claimed he took to heart: "Some of those who envied me added that I owed it all to my brother. . . . I knew full well how true it was."

Perhaps because of the pain of adjusting to a disconcertingly modern city, the pressures of feeling overshadowed yet again by the fame of his brother, or a sense that his linguistic resources as a Yiddish writer were out of joint with his unfamiliar American surroundings, Singer's output dwindled in the late 1930s. The sense of dread and paralysis described in his account of writing *The Sinning Messiah* intensified as he struggled to adapt to life in the United States. His autobiographical novel *Warshe 1914–1918* (*Warsaw 1914–1918*), a fragment of which was serialized in a Warsaw newspaper shortly after his departure from Poland, remained unfinished. In 1937, the usually prolific Singer contributed a mere four stories and sketches to the *Forward*, and by the middle of the year he had stopped writing fiction altogether. His most significant project in the late 1930s was his translation from German into Yiddish of *From Moscow to Jerusalem*, the autobiography of Leon Glaser, an official of Kerensky's government in Russia who later immigrated to Palestine. Singer became involved with an unsuccessful theatrical endeavor during the summer of 1938, and he spent several weeks directing English-language rehearsals of I. L. Peretz's play *A Night in the Old Marketplace* at Grine Felder (Green Fields), an arts colony in the Catskills. Despite the producers' hopes of bringing the play to New York City, the production was never staged.

30. Photograph of Singer's wife, Alma, taken at Bloomingdale's.

Singer had visited the Catskills the previous summer, vacationing on a small farm not far from Grine Felder in Mountaindale, N.Y. Decades later, he drew upon memories of Mountaindale to write "The Yearning Heifer," a story that opens with a gloomy montage of dilapidated houses in a menacing "wilderness" and concludes with an ending resembling those of several other stories, most notably "Short Friday" and "The Spinoza of Market Street," in which eternal mysteries are evoked with grace and understated awe:

31. In the summer of 1937, while vacationing in Mountaindale, N.Y., Singer met Alma Haimann Wassermann (*second from left*), who had fled Germany in 1936. Singer and Alma married in 1940. Alma's mother is second from right.

32. Singer with Alma and her first husband, Walter Wassermann, and their daughter Inga.

There was no moon, but the summer night was bright. Fireflies lit up in the thickets. Frogs croaked, crickets chirped. The night rained meteors. I could make out the whitish luminous band which was the Milky Way. The sky, like the earth, could not rest. It yearned with a cosmic yearning for something which would take myriads of light-years to achieve.

Singer met his future wife, Alma Haimann Wassermann, in Mountaindale that summer. The daughter of an affluent German-Jewish textile merchant and, like Singer, a recent immigrant, she had settled with her husband and two children in Washington Heights at the northern end of Manhattan. Her native language was German; she did not read Yiddish. Of her first encounter with Singer, she recalled that he was "young, slim, blond, almost bald, had very blue eyes and seemed completely lost or disoriented as far as finding the dining room, his room or even the road outside. . . . We learned that he was a budding writer, that he had so far written one book and that it was a good book." Soon Singer was romantically involved with her, and in the middle of a blizzard on Valentine's Day in 1940, not long after Alma and her husband divorced, Singer and Alma were married in a civil ceremony at Brooklyn City Hall. The couple moved into a small apartment on Ocean Avenue in Brooklyn, and Alma began working in the women's fashion division of the Arnold Constable store on Fifth

33. Envelope addressed to "D. Segal," one of the pseudonyms under which Singer wrote for the *Forward*. Reserving "Yitskhok Bashevis" for his literary works and "Y. Varshavski" for his reviews, more thoughtful articles, and bellelettristic sketches (including those collected in *In My Father's Court*), Singer used "D. Segal" to sign his tabloid journalism. Among the first "D. Segal" articles published in 1942 were "The Latest Fashion: Trial Marriages" and "She Had Many Loves in Her Life But Quietly Killed Off Every One."

JEWISH DAILY FORWARD

World's Largest Jewish Daily

175 EAST BROADWAY

NEW YORK

September 11, 1935

Hon. Commissioner of Immigration,
Ellis Island, New York

Dear Sir:

Mr. Icek-Hersz Zynger of Warsaw, a novelist and writer, now here on a visit in this country, has been assigned by us to prepare and write an extensive serial to be published in our newspaper.

The serial will require Mr. Zynger's presence in this country for about one year for the purpose of research work and the preparation of copy. His special training and outstanding gifts in this field make his services to us indispensable.

We therefore would greatly appreciate it if you would grant Mr. Zynger an extension for one year so that he may be able to fulfill his assignment.

Respectfully,

Harry Rogoff

Managing Editor

THE GATEWAY TO THE JEWISH MARKET

JEWISH DAILY FORWARD

World's Largest Jewish Daily

175 EAST BROADWAY
NEW YORK
GRamercy 5-8000

YOUR EARNINGS FOR THE YEAR 1942
AMOUNTED TO THE SUM OF $ *3619.51*

IT IS YOUR DUTY TO PAY YOUR INCOME
TAX EARLY AND OFTEN.

34 (*above*). Letter to Commissioner of Immigration at Ellis Island requesting one-year extension for Singer's visa on behalf of the *Jewish Daily Forward*.

35 (*right*). Earnings statement for 1942, totaling $3,619.51. "It is your duty to pay your income tax early and often."

Avenue, the first of several department-store jobs as a salesperson and buyer. The following year they rented an apartment on West 103rd Street in Manhattan and moved to the Upper West Side, the neighborhood where they would live for more than four decades.

Although Singer continued to be blocked as a fiction writer, he was now regularly writing for the *Forward* under the pen names "Yitskhok Varshavski" (i.e., "Isaac from Warsaw") and, later and less frequently, "D. Segal." His short articles ranged from human-interest stories ("What Studies Have Uncovered About Talented Children") to summaries of current and historical events ("English Jews Fought as Heroes, Died as Martyrs in York Pogrom") to general philosophical and social observations ("Can a Person Change?"; "Shyness—A Plague Affecting Large and Small, Rich and Poor"; "Why Men and Women Divorce—No Rules But the Cases Are Interesting"). Distinct from his more literary works, which were usually published under the name "Bashevis," these columns were nonetheless a boon to Singer at a troubled point in his career. With their populist concerns, offbeat facts, and speculations about the ethics of everyday life, these articles assured Singer a regular audience among the *Forward*'s readership. Due to his work as a columnist, the newspaper hired him as a salaried member of its staff in the early 1940s. His steady work as a writer for the *Forward* provided the security for him to pursue the ambitious series of stories that ended his drought as a fiction writer. In the process of crafting these tales, Singer sealed his mastery of the short-story form.

36. Morris Kreitman (later known as Maurice Carr), Hinde Esther's only child. Raised in England, Kreitman edited the anthology *Jewish Short Stories of Today* (1938), which included his translation of an excerpt from *Satan in Goray*, the first appearance of Singer's work in English. Kreitman's anthology was the only book containing works by Singer, Israel Joshua, and Hinde Esther published while all three writers were alive.

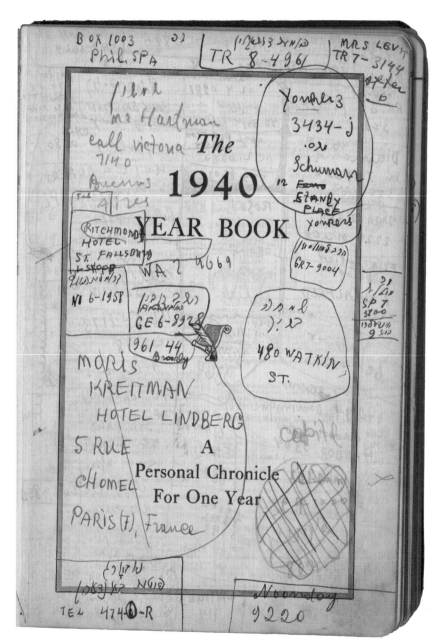

37. The title page of Singer's 1940 daily planner. Among the many scrawled notations is a Paris address for Morris Kreitman.

Jonathan Safran Foer: Subtlety is generally regarded as one of principle virtues of good writing. The better the writing, the more it suggests, evokes, resonates—the less is *said*. But that's not Singer's game. What I'm always struck by, when reading his stories and novels, is just how much he actually *says*: he says the things that could go unsaid; he says the things we already know. But it's in no way redundant or unnecessary, and it certainly isn't the mark of bad writing. It's his genius, and the effect is thrilling.

Singer is the only writer with the power to make me blush. My face isn't responding to his sexiness (although he has plenty of that), and it isn't because of his irreverence (which he's also got in abundance). It's his frankness. He writes about "fate" and "love" and "death"—he actually uses those words—as if no one ever taught him that saying exactly what you mean—talking about what you're talking about—leaves you with no protection. It's so easy to hide behind ambiguity. It's so hard to fess up. Many times I have finished a Singer story and thought, "I can't believe he actually wrote that." It's the vulnerability that I love. Another word for it might be bravery.

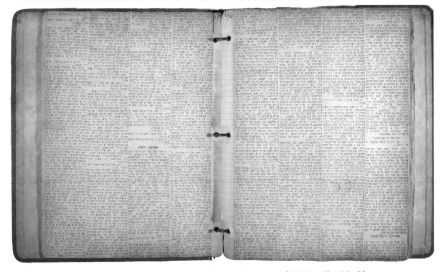

38. Singer's scrapbook containing the *Forward*'s serialization of *Di familye Mushkat* (*The Family Moskat*). After it appeared from late 1945 to 1948, the novel was published in two divergent versions, in Yiddish and in English translation, in 1950.

Breakthrough
1942–1950

THE FIVE stories Singer published in 1943—later translated into English as "The Unseen," "Zeidlus the Pope," "The Destruction of Kreshev," "From the Diary of One Not Born," and "Two Corpses Go Dancing"—are each told by a demonic narrator, usually the devil himself. "I am the Primeval Snake, the Evil One, Satan," runs the opening of "The Destruction of Kreshev," a declaration echoed in each of the stories. "The cabala refers to me as Samael and the Jews sometimes call me merely, 'that one.'" At first glance, because these stories chart the ruin of men and women through weaknesses that are easily exploited by the forces of evil, they might be read as cautionary tales, fables meant to encourage moral vigilance. In "Zeidlus the Pope," the brilliant scholar Zeidel falls victim to his vanity and, convinced he will eventually be named pope, foolishly converts to Christianity. In "The Unseen," the wealthy grain merchant Nathan Jozefover's fondness for indulging the pleasures of the flesh leads to his ensnarement in an adulterous liaison and his transformation into a wasted, shrunken pauper. Doomed by all-too-human failings, these characters are punished for acts they seem destined to commit. That such figures are chastised for their vices reveals a conservative strand in Singer's fictional method, a link to traditional storytelling. But the moralizing in these tales is undermined by a modern element, irrational and anarchic, that employs the supernaturalism of the folktale in an original and disturbing fashion. In Singer's stories of the early 1940s, a demonic voice has usurped the authority of the traditional storyteller. Instead of expressing folk truths and communal wisdom, this voice takes fiendish delight as the stories' characters are tormented by urges and fantasies that effortlessly master them.

Writing during a time when the Jews were being exterminated in Europe, Singer staged the triumph of irrational forces in his stories. He imagined scenes of catastrophic violence: at the conclusion of "The Destruction of Kreshev," the village is ravaged by fire, and "since it was bitter cold at the time and many people were left without a roof over their heads, quite a few fell ill, a plague followed, men, women and children perished, and Kreshev was truly destroyed. To this day the town has remained small and poor; it has never been rebuilt to its former size." At the end of "The Unseen," the history of Frampol unfolds in reverse, taking shape as a dreamlike backwards march toward a scene of primal aggression:

> Then the building and builders vanished, and he saw a group of people, barefooted, bearded, wild-eyed, with crosses in their hands, lead a Jew to the gallows. Though the black-bearded young man cried heart-rendingly, they dragged him on, tied in ropes. Bells were ringing; the people in the streets ran away and hid. It was midday, but it grew dark as the day of an eclipse of the sun. Finally, the young man cried out: "Shema Yisroel, the Lord our God, the Lord is One," and was left hanging, his tongue lolling out. His legs swayed for a long time, and hosts of crows flew overhead, cawing hoarsely.

From the opening pages of *Satan in Goray*, Singer had confronted the history of murderous anti-Semitism in Europe. Living in safety in the United States, he was profoundly affected by World War II—he lost contact with his mother and brother Moishe in 1939 and was told some time after the war's end that they were deported by the Soviets to Kazakhstan, where they were reported to have frozen to death. But the destruction of the Jews in Europe would not become a dominant theme in his work for some time. When asked to contribute to a 1943 issue of the journal *Di tsukunft* devoted to the catastrophe overseas, Singer submitted

39. Building at 175 East Broadway housing the *Jewish Daily Forward* offices, 1927.

the essay "Concerning Yiddish Literature in Poland." Far more detached in tone than other contributions to the issue, the essay combined an account of the Yiddish P.E.N. Club in Warsaw with a severely critical evaluation of the predicament of Yiddish writing in Poland between the world wars. It was a bleak, unsparing assessment: modern Yiddish writers, rejecting tradition for chimeric secular ideologies, had created a literature that was "godly without a god, worldly without a world." As for the contemporary situation, the essay's terse concluding sentences about the Yiddish writer bereft of a culture to sustain him— "His characters are dead. Their language has been silenced. All that he has to draw from are memories"—suggest that for Singer, the Nazi genocide possessed a terrible finality well before the war's end. In what was almost certainly a nod to *Satan in Goray*, Singer casts the eradication of Jewish culture in Poland as a historical inevitability: "Long before the Nazis entered Poland, the Yiddish writer perceived the scent of the Middle Ages, of slaughter and martyrdom. He inherited the great solitude of the Jew on earth and the eternal forces that were shaping his destiny.

40. Members of the prepress department at the *Forward* preparing plates for the newspaper, 1927.

The better the writer, the more boldly these feelings were expressed in his work."

America was a refuge from the slaughter, but it still presented a fundamental quandary for the Yiddish writer, a dilemma that had crippled Singer's ability to create fiction for several years. In 1943, now writing some of his best stories, he outlined the situation of the immigrant Yiddish writer in the essay "Problems of Yiddish Prose in America." His pessimistic outlook was intended to be controversial—the editors of the magazine *Svive*, where the essay was published, included the disclaimer that Singer's views were not their own. As a means of expression, Singer wrote, Yiddish is best suited to describing the distant past. Neologisms and words imported from foreign languages to describe contemporary reality sound jarring, tawdry, debased. "Americanisms reek of foreignness, of cheap glitter, of impermanence. The result is that the better Yiddish writers avoid treating American life, and they are subjectively (aesthetically) right to do so." Even the old words of the mother tongue begin to seem absurd in the new environment. The uprooted Yiddish writer finds his very language slipping away from him. As well as shedding light on his difficulties writing fiction during his first years in the United States, "Problems of Yiddish Prose in America" offers insights into Singer's attraction to the historical novel and stories set in a mythic past. As for the country he adopted as his home, except for the closing section of the story "The Little Shoemakers," Singer avoided writing about America in his fiction until the 1950s.

Early in 1944, Singer received a shock that would have far-reaching consequences. On February 10, at the age of 50, Israel Joshua Singer

ISRAEL SINGER DIES; YIDDISH AUTHOR, 50

Wrote Novels of Polish Jews, Notably 'Brothers Ashkenazi' —Successful Playwright

Israel Joshua Singer, Yiddish author and playwright, whose works were translated into many languages, died yesterday of a heart attack in his home at 258 Riverside Drive. He was 50 years old.

His novels, which dealt with Polish Jews, included "The Brothers As⸍⸍⸍ ⸍'" "Yoshe Kalb" and "T⸍⸍⸍ ⸍ky," dramati-produced by

⸍ation by ⸍rothers ⸍n 1936, TIMES , Ralph story of ⸍wo Polish ⸍d and elo-⸍le piece of

⸍43 ⸍uced

41, 42. Obituary for Israel Joshua Singer from *The New York Times*, February 11, 1944.

died of a heart attack at his home on Riverside Drive in Manhattan. For the rest of his career, the younger Singer maintained a posture of reverence toward Israel Joshua, dedicating two books to his memory and referring to his older brother as his "master." But the unexpected death that caused him to grieve as a brother had a liberating effect on the man who had always been regarded as the lesser of the two writers. Not long after his brother's death, Singer began researching and outlining the sprawling realist novel *Di familye Mushkat* (*The Family Moskat*), a chronicle of Jewish Warsaw spanning several generations and, broadly speaking, an exploration of the effects of modernity and secularism on Polish Jews. Of all Singer's works, *The Family Moskat* most resembles a book Israel Joshua might have written.

Before throwing himself completely into the novel, however, Singer continued to write stories set in towns in the Lublin region of Poland: Frampol, Lapschitz, Turbin. One of these stories, published in 1945, is arguably Singer's most famous tale. "Gimpel the Fool" inverts the formula of stories like "Zeidlus the Pope" and "The Unseen," with their sly demonic narrators cackling over the inevitable demise of morally vulnerable characters. This story is narrated by the gullible fool Gimpel, the laughingstock of Frampol, an orphan and apparent simpleton who is cuckolded by his wife.

43. Knopf advertisement for English translation of *The Family Moskat*, 1950, linking Singer's book with Israel Joshua's "warm, rich, and lusty" novel, *The Brothers Ashkenazi*. After rejecting pen names such as "Bashevis (Isaac Singer)" and "Isaac Singer Bashevis," Singer published the novel as "Isaac Bashevis Singer," the name he would use to sign all his works in English.

Over the course of the story, Gimpel is revealed to be an upright and exemplary man. "All Frampol refreshed its spirits because of my trouble and grief. However, I resolved that I would always believe what I was told. What's the good of *not* believing? Today it's your wife you don't believe; tomorrow it's God Himself you won't take stock in." The evil force that has its way with so many of Singer's characters cannot defeat Gimpel's guilelessness and trust in God. Although the story can be regarded as a parable affirming humility and simple virtue, "Gimpel the Fool" assumes a provocative stance in relation to Singer's other stories—are those urges that take shape as demons, devils, and dybbuks really so easily thwarted?—and to contemporary events. The clarity of the storytelling leads to murkier questions about faith, human illusions, and divine justice.

The composition of *The Family Moskat*, published in installments in the *Forward* from 1945 to 1948 and broadcast as a weekly radio serial on the New York Yiddish radio station

44. Letter from Alfred Knopf to Singer dated August 25, 1949, requesting that Singer follow the recommendation of Knopf editors to cut and revise *The Family Moskat*. Knopf pointed out that Singer's "dear brother" Israel Joshua's *The Brothers Ashkenazi* was trimmed for publication in English translation in 1936.

Cables:
KNOPF NEW YORK
Telephones:
PLAZA 3-4761

BORZOI BOOKS

Alfred A Knopf *Incorporated*

501 *Madison Avenue* NEW YORK

August 25, 1949

Dear Mr. Singer,

I must confess that I am greatly disturbed by Mr. Weinstock's report of his last conversation with you following your receipt of his long letter of August 19. Four of us have now read carefully the manuscript of THE FAMILY MUSKAT and I am one of the four. I agree heartily with every one that this book is likely to have a very poor chance indeed with the American bookseller if it is not substantially cut. I realize how painful an author finds such surgery and how easily and freely his blood flows; and sometimes I am very reluctant to press my point. But in your case there is such unanimity of opinion and I am, myself, so sure that my advisors are correct in their judgment, that I must beg of you to give weight to my judgment in a matter of this kind.

As a matter of fact, when we made our agreement with you for this book, it was my understanding that the question of cutting would be decided finally by Mr. Gross and that there would be no appeal from his decision. I had just such an arrangement with your dear brother in the case of the BROTHERS ASHKENAZI. There Maurice Samuel was the judge. Of course one cannot guarantee results in advance of publication, but certainly your brother had no reason in the end to feel that he had made a mistake in following our advice and Samuel's in cutting very considerably the BROTHERS ASHKENAZI.

There is no reason at all why THE FAMILY MUSKAT should not be made from the point of view of the American reader into a very much

WEVD, absorbed most of Singer's energies as a writer during the late 1940s. The novel was also translated into English, a project that was beset with difficulties from the start. Its first translator, Abraham Gross, died before his English version was completed. His daughter Nancy finished the translation, which was submitted to Alfred A. Knopf for publication in 1949. Herbert Weinstock, an editor at Knopf, read the typescript and advised that Singer make extensive cuts. At first, Singer refused to alter the novel, prompting a protracted rift. Alfred Knopf intervened. "I agree heartily with everyone," Knopf wrote to Singer, "that this book is likely to have a very poor chance indeed with the American bookseller if it is not substantially cut." Resenting the publisher's interference, Singer nevertheless agreed to make substantive changes to *The Family Moskat*. More than 100 pages were omitted from the English translation, including the final chapter of the original version. The difference between the two endings is telling: the English translation ends as a Nazi bombardment pummels Warsaw, concluding with the bleak words, "Death is the Messiah. That's the real truth." The original Yiddish ending is more hopeful, describing a mass exodus to Palestine and closing with the ancient words of Moses, "Yours is the final victory. Unto you will come the Messiah."

The Family Moskat garnered favorable notices in a handful of newspapers—bundled with reviews of eight other "titles of interest" in *The New York Times*, it received respectful praise for its "throbbing vitality"—but it was not a commercial success and soon went out of print for more than a decade. Singer remained unhappy about Knopf's interference, and Knopf, for its part, was skeptical about Singer's appeal to an American audience beyond the readers of the *Forward*. When Singer submitted a lengthy excerpt from his novel *The Estate* to Knopf in 1951, the firm acknowledged little more than polite interest. If he had hoped to match the crossover success that his brother had achieved through the English translations of his novels *Yoshe Kalb* and *The Brothers Ashkenazi*, he was sorely disappointed. *The Family Moskat* receded into obscurity, and for all but his Yiddish readership he remained unknown as a writer in America. Soon, with the assistance of a handful of influential writers and intellectuals, this was about to change.

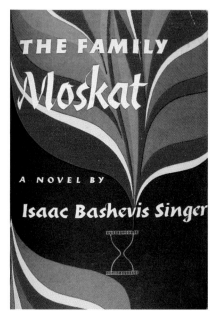

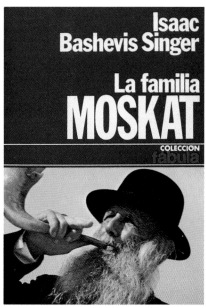

45 (*above left*). Dust jacket of the 1950 Knopf edition of *The Family Moskat*. After modestly favorable reviews and lukewarm sales, it went out of print until its reissue in 1965.

46, 47, 48. In the 1970s and 1980s, when Singer's international fame was at its height, the novel was widely translated. Pictured here are the Spanish, German, and Yugoslavian editions.

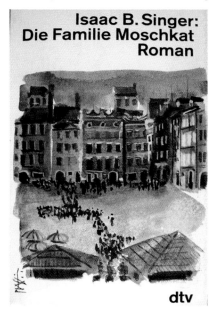

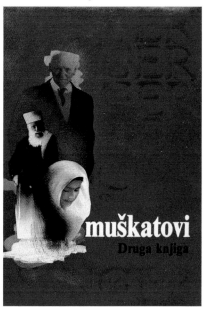

Cynthia Ozick: On one flank Singer is a trickster, a prankster, a Loki, a Puck. His themes are lust, greed, pride, obsession, misfortune, unreason, the oceanic surprises of the mind's underside, the fiery cauldron of the self, the assaults of time and place. His stories offer no "epiphanies" and no pious resolutions. Their plenitudes chiefly serve undefended curiosity, the gossip's lure of what-comes-next. Singer's stories have plots that unravel not because they are old-fashioned—they are mostly originals and have few recognizable modes other than their own—but because they contain the whole human world of affliction, error, quagmire, pain, calamity, catastrophe, woe: things happen; life is an ambush, a snare; one's fate can never be predicted. His driven, mercurial processions of predicaments and transmogrifications are limitless, a cornucopia of invention.

Because he cracks open decorum to find lust, because he peers past convention into the pit of fear, Singer in the past has been condemned by other Yiddish writers outraged by his seemingly pagan subject matter, his superstitious villagers, his daring leaps into gnostic furies. The moral grain of feeling that irradiates the mainstream aspirations of Yiddish literature has always been a kind of organic extension of Talmudic ethical ideals: family, devotion, community probity—self-respect and respect for others—the stringent expectations of high public civility and indefatigable integrity, the dream of messianic betterment. In Singer, much of this seems absent or overlooked or simply mocked; it is as if he has willed the crashing-down of traditional Jewish sanity and sensibility.

In fact, he betrays nothing and no one, least of all Jewish idealism. That is the meaning of his imps and demons: that human character, left to itself, is drawn to cleanliness of heart: that human motivation, on its own, is attracted to clarity and valor. Here is Singer's other flank, and it is the broader one. The goblin cunning leads straight to this: Singer is a moralist. He tells us that it is natural to be good, and unholy to go astray. It is only when Lilith creeps in, or Samael, or Ketev Mriri, or the sons of Asmodeus, that evil and impurity are kindled. It is the inhuman, the antihuman forces that are to blame for harms and sorrows. Surely these imps must be believed in; they may have Satan's tell-tale geeselike feet, but their difficult, shaming, lubricious urges are terrestrially familiar. Yet however lamentably known they are, Singer's demons are intruders, invaders, no welcome part of ourselves. They are "psychology"; and history; and terror; above all, obsessive will. If he believes in them, so, unwillingly but genuinely, do we.

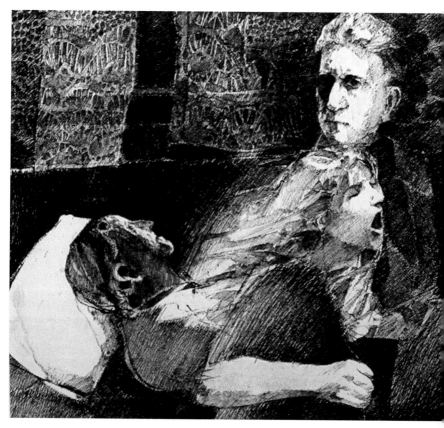

49. Illustration by Paul Giovanopoulos that accompanied Singer's story "The Lecture" in *Playboy*, December 1967.

American Lights,
American Shadows
1951–1958

SINGER WAS never in danger of losing his *Forward* readers, but his eventual rise to international prominence began with the translation of "Gimpel the Fool" into English in 1953. The critic Irving Howe and the Yiddish poet Eliezer Greenberg had read the tale while putting together an English-language anthology of Yiddish stories, and then convinced a somewhat reluctant Saul Bellow—who was busy finishing his novel *The Adventures of Augie March* and teaching at Princeton—to prepare a translation. The English version was completed in a long afternoon session in Greenberg's East 19th Street apartment, with Greenberg reading Singer's Yiddish text and Howe looking on "in a state of high enchantment" as Bellow sat at a typewriter and translated from Greenberg's dictation. Bellow's rendering of "Gimpel the Fool" shares the buoyant energy and verbal deftness of his *Augie March*, and in passages Singer's deceptively straightforward tale of shtetl life sounds, in Bellow's version, quite American, cast in a brisk colloquial idiom that one might hear on the streets of Chicago or New York ("I had seven names in all: imbecile, donkey, flax-head, dope, glump, ninny, and fool"; "that was no go either"). Bellow's efforts on Singer's behalf did not, however, lead to a friendship or further collaboration between the two writers and eventual Nobel laureates, who maintained a rather wary distance in the years that followed.

On Howe's recommendation, "Gimpel the Fool" was published in *Partisan Review* in May 1953, and the next year the story was included, along with "The Little Shoemakers," in Howe and Greenberg's anthology *A Treasury of Yiddish Stories*. Howe later described his first reading of "Gimpel the Fool" as a revelatory moment, an occasion of rare discovery: "How often does a critic encounter a major new writer?" The identification of Singer as a "new writer"—he was now nearly fifty, and had published thousands of pages of fiction in Yiddish—was not merely a reference to Howe's fresh acquaintance with Singer's work. For Howe, Greenberg, and the writers and critics affiliated with *Partisan Review* who embraced him in the 1950s, Singer embodied a novel and seductive cluster of contradictions: he seemed a modern yet anachronistic figure, a folk writer with a cosmopolitan outlook, an exile who had never really left his (now liquidated) home. As his fame grew, Singer enjoyed dismissing most twentieth-century writers and their pretensions, avant-garde experiments, and political enthusiasms, but it's worth recalling that he was first celebrated by English-speaking critics in America as a master of modernism. For the editors of *Partisan Review*'s 1954 anthology *More Stories in the Modern Manner*, it made perfect sense to include "Gimpel the Fool" alongside works by Proust, James Agee, and Alberto Moravia. But because he used religious orthodoxy as literary material rather than a set of beliefs and practices to ignore, satirize, or reject outright, Singer's modernism carried a distinctive accent. "Deeply learned in Hasidic and cabalistic lore," wrote Howe and Greenberg with perhaps a shade of hyperbole in *A Treasury of Yiddish Stories*, Singer "brings to play upon Jewish life of several centuries ago—as upon contemporary Jewish life—a mind that reveres and delights in religious customs and emotions, yet is simultaneously drenched in modern psychological skepticism."

Tales such as "Gimpel the Fool," "The Little Shoemakers," and "From the Diary of One Not Born" (published in translation in *Partisan Review* in 1954) appealed to critics like Howe and Greenberg because these stories bring together tradition and modernity in sophisticated and unexpected ways, much like the works of Franz Kafka. But unlike Kafka, whose idiosyncratic German exudes alienation and inner torment at every turn, and modernist writers of Jewish extraction as

PARTISAN REVIEW

MAY-JUNE, 1953

DELMORE SCHWARTZ
An Inside Story

LUDWIG MARCUSE
European Anti-Americanism

ELIZABETH HARDWICK
The Subjection of Women

ISAAC BASHEVIS SINGER
Gimpel the Fool (a story)

VICTOR ERLICH
Formalist Criticism in Russia

SAUL BELLOW
Hemingway and the Image of Man

SONYA RUDIKOFF
Colette at Eighty

Poems and reviews by Louis Kronenberger, Steven Marcus, Elizabeth Pollet, Ralph Gilbert Ross, Vernon Watkins, Pearce Young

75¢

50. Cover of *Partisan Review*, May–June 1953, which included Saul Bellow's translation of Singer's story "Gimpel the Fool."

varied as Isaac Babel, Henry Roth, and Bruno Schulz (at the time little known), Singer wrote in Yiddish, the vernacular "jargon" of Ashkenazi Jews. Linguistically Singer was a direct link to the Eastern European Jewish world devastated by the Nazis and Stalin's Soviet Union, and he evoked this annihilated world in rich detail and with the authority of a wise, skeptical emigré. At the same time Singer's American advocates were drawn to his lean, unsentimental prose style, a departure from the norm of much Yiddish writing, which indulged in rhetoric that seemed, at least if judged by reigning Flaubertian standards of precision and exactitude, florid and excessive.

Singer's interest in the demonic brought him into the circle of modernism. Fascinated by the eruption of irrational urges and their destructive consequences, Singer shares one of the telltale preoccupations of the modern artist. But while his stories seem to illuminate the troubling lessons of Freud, they carry no trace of the seminar, lecture hall, or analyst's office; indeed, they deliver the uncanny sense that Freud's psychological insights are already embedded in the folkloric idiom that Singer made his own by unearthing its infernal undercurrents. And yet, countervailing his exploration of unbridled irrationality is a revulsion to nihilism in all its forms—thus the man who wrote the story "The Wife-Killer," a grotesque tale of primal havoc between the sexes, is also the author of the parable of goodness and probity, "Gimpel the Fool." To cite yet another contradiction at the core of his achievement: Singer is at once a transgressive iconoclast and a deeply humane writer.

In time, Singer's arrival on the American literary scene as an important Yiddish writer—in effect, the *only* Yiddish writer familiar to Americans who did not read Yiddish—through the publication of "Gimpel the Fool" in *Partisan Review* became part of the legend of his success. Offhand comments in interviews and in journalistic profiles often gave the impression that the appearance of "Gimpel the Fool" in English transformed Singer into an overnight literary sensation. This isn't quite true; compared with his wide readership in the 1960s and 1970s, when his stories were regularly featured in such mass-circulation magazines as *Mademoiselle*, *Harper's*, *Playboy*, and *The New Yorker*, the audience of *Partisan Review* was relatively small. But its readers were an influential group of writers, editors, and publishers. Cecil Hemley, publisher and co-founder of Noonday Press, admired "Gimpel the Fool" when he read it in *Partisan*

Review, and when the two men met not long afterward they became fast friends. Soon Noonday agreed to bring out Jacob Sloan's translation of *Satan in Goray*. The novel was published in English in 1955, and the collection *Gimpel the Fool and Other Stories* followed two years later.

Singer's relationship with Noonday and Farrar, Straus & Cudahy (later Farrar, Straus & Giroux), the firm that acquired Noonday in the late 1950s, was far more agreeable than his troubled dealings with Knopf. From the beginning, he was regarded as a prized author. Hemley himself collaborated with Singer to prepare English versions of many stories and the novel *The Slave*; his wife, Elaine Gottlieb, also worked on English translations of stories and several novels. Singer's stature at Noonday and Farrar, Straus & Giroux guaranteed a mutually beneficial arrangement between author and publisher for the rest of his career, as Singer, drawing from a fund of his writings from the *Forward* and other Yiddish sources, published story collections and serialized novels in translation at a rapid pace, averaging nearly a book a year. Perhaps the most important effect of the publication of "Gimpel the Fool" in *Partisan Review* was its role in initiating Singer's relationship with Hemley and Noonday, which in turn led to Singer's long tenure as one of Farrar, Straus & Giroux's most prominent writers.

As Singer's life with Alma on Central Park West assumed a regular routine during the 1950s, two events recalled some of the family turmoil that he had left behind in Europe. The death of his sister Hinde Esther in 1954 marked the passing of his last surviving sibling. They had last seen each other six years before when Singer had visited her in England to introduce her to Alma. Now Singer was the only living member of the Krochmalna Street household. The street itself had been reduced to rubble along with the rest of Warsaw's Jewish quarter during World War II. Singer's closest living relative was his son, Israel, whom he had not seen since leaving Poland. But in 1955, after twenty years of separation, father and son were reunited when Israel (who adopted the last name "Zamir," Hebrew for songbird) traveled from Haifa to New York to work on behalf of his kibbutz. The meeting was chronicled by both men, by Singer in his autobiographical story "The Son" and by Zamir in a 1970 essay published in the Tel Aviv newspaper *Al ha-Mishmar* (and, after Singer's death, in Zamir's memoir *Journey to My Father, Isaac Bashevis Singer*). Although their relationship was not without its difficulties, the two men were eventually able to forge a bond from "what started as a failed father-son relationship and ended in a mature friendship," as Zamir wrote in his memoir. Zamir translated many of Singer's short stories into Hebrew, and he was on hand in Stockholm when Singer was awarded the Nobel Prize in 1978.

In the mid-1950s, Singer looked to his past to begin creating the vast corpus of autobiographical writings about his youth and early manhood that would eventually span several volumes. The first of these efforts, published in the *Forward* in 1955 under his "Varshavski" pseudonym, was a series of sketches about his father's rabbinical court in Warsaw. These vignettes, many which were translated and collected eleven years later in the volume *In My Father's Court*, struck a popular chord, and they remain some of his most beloved works. In 1957, eight episodes from the series were dramatized by the Folksbiene (People's Theater) on Manhattan's Lower East Side, the first of many stage adaptations of Singer's stories. Singer also wrote sketches about his grandfather's rabbinical court in Bilgoray and his time at the Warsaw Yiddish Writers' Club. These works were later joined by a serialized memoir, "From the Old and New

51. Israel Zamir, Eilat, 1949. In the story "The Son," Singer's account of his reunion with his son after a twenty-year separation, he wrote: "He had sent me one photograph taken when he had served in the army and fought the Arabs. But the picture was blurred, and in addition he was wearing a uniform. Only now, as the first passengers began to come down, did it occur to me that I did not have a clear image of what my son looked like. Was he tall? Was he short? Had his blond hair turned dark with the years? This son's arrival in America pushed me back to an epoch which I had thought of as already belonging to eternity. He was emerging out of the past like a phantom."

Home" and the three volumes of "an autobiography I never intend to write" collected in English under the title *Love and Exile*, as well as many autobiographical novels about the Warsaw years, *Shosha*, *The Certificate*, and *Scum* among them.

Shortly after completing *The Family Moskat*, Singer began writing *Der hoyf* (*The Court*, published many years later in English translation as the two volumes *The Manor* and *The Estate*), a massive historical narrative set in nineteenth-century Poland. The novel that followed was a journey into new territory: having now spent two decades in New York, Singer was finally ready to tackle the subject of the United States. *Shadows on the Hudson*, serialized in the *Forward* from January 1957 to January 1958 and not translated into English until after his death, was Singer's first sustained, substantive treatment of his adopted country in his fiction. At once a tragicomic soap opera and a haunted, often caustic evaluation of Jewish emigré life in America, *Shadows on*

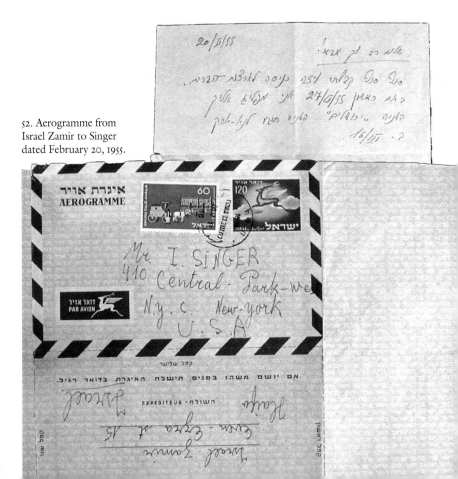

52. Aerogramme from Israel Zamir to Singer dated February 20, 1955.

the Hudson combines a narrative technique indebted to nineteenth-century masters—and in the grand nineteenth-century manner, a destructive episode of adultery propels the plot—with a pessimistic indictment of twentieth-century barbarism. Set in the late 1940s, the recent atrocities of the Holocaust loom large, but as a refuge for Jews the United States offers little more than physical sanctuary from the European slaughter and the opportunity to make—and lose—one's fortune. *Shadows on the Hudson* puts forth the view that American Jews will share the destiny of other ethnic groups and become wholly deracinated. Grein, one of the novel's central characters, reflects on the fate of his children, American-born Jack and Anita:

> Once again the train emerged from underground and ran above Brooklyn back yards: tiny houses, small stony gardens, and streetlamps that merely deepened the night gloom. All kinds of ethnic groups lived and raised children here: Jews, Italians, Poles, and Irish; black people and yellow people. In these dwellings, cultures flickered and died out. Here children grew up without any heritage, like Jack, like Anita. Their spiritual fathers were stock Hollywood characters, their literature trashy novels and the tabloid press. How long could all this last?

For Grein, America is at best a cipher, hinting at unchanging human verities beneath its ephemeral signs of decadence:

> The wider America with which Grein came into contact was just as complicated as he was himself. He would never understand it properly. America remained for him the one country in the world where people walked with their heads held high, yet he could see that behind all individual differences the eternal human tragedy remained constant. People loved each other and loathed each other, took risks and were afraid. Each of them kept looking for a stable, permanent support upon which to lean, but power craftier than human beings continually snatched these away, creating a perpetual crisis.

Of course Grein is not Singer, merely one of his characters. But the more reflective characters in *Shadows on the Hudson* express grave misgivings about the United States, whereas those who embrace America wholeheartedly tend to be savagely drawn caricatures—a group of vacationing Jewish-Americans in Miami are the target of especially cutting satire—or, as in the case of the actor Yasha Kotik, cunning, slippery figures who lack moral bearings. But ultimately, here as elsewhere in Singer's writings, America possesses an unnerving sense of unreality, as if for the Jewish exile the United States is less an actual place than a spectral borderland between the realm of the dead and the shattered world of those who escaped the genocide. Grein is most often described as a walking corpse. Memories of obliterated places cue dreams or eerily supplant real locales: a snowfall transforms Manhattan into a ghostly projection of Warsaw; a train ride through upstate New York suggests a journey through Siberian wastes. The American setting recedes as the psychic landscape of exile exerts its pressures.

Although *Shadows on the Hudson* was known only to Singer's *Forward* readers during his lifetime, many of its themes and concerns are echoed in works later translated into English, such as the stories "A Wedding in Brownsville" and "The Cafeteria." When he chose to be, Singer could be quite forthright about what he regarded as hollow American values and the shallow promise of assimilation—though he frequently expressed gratitude for the opportunities that America had offered him as well. Writing novels and tales set in New York (and occasionally Miami Beach), an "American" Singer emerged in the 1960s and 1970s to complement the storyteller who seemed a last remnant of the Ashkenazi Jewish culture destroyed by the Nazis. But Singer's views as explored in his fiction were somewhat at variance with the advent of an increasingly visible persona: grandfatherly, witty, exotic and charming, an ambassador from a vanished world. As he achieved ever greater renown—awarded prizes, feted at home and abroad, eagerly sought out for lectures and interviews—the writer and the literary celebrity became overlapping but often divergent aspects of the same man, the mysterious, evasive figure known to the world as Isaac Bashevis Singer.

53. Singer in Washington Square Park, Greenwich Village, 1966.

54. A page from one of Singer's notebooks. "Singer was always writing, usually on pads of lined paper," remarked Simon Weber, longtime editor of the *Jewish Daily Forward*. "He could sit anywhere and write. In a car, in a crowded room—anywhere." Singer noted that he would grow irritated writing Yiddish across pages with ruled left-hand margins. "If there wouldn't be this red line," he quipped, "I might really have become a genius."

Making It

1959–1977

SINGER ONCE claimed that he preferred writing stories to novels because the short-story form brought perfection within reach. Although he continued to publish novels at an impressive rate—*The Magician of Lublin* appeared in English in 1960, followed by *The Slave* in 1962—it was above all as a short-story writer that Singer was lionized in the United States. After *Gimpel the Fool and Other Stories*, the collections *The Spinoza of Market Street* and *Short Friday* served up an embarrassment of riches: "The Man Who Came Back," "Taibele and Her Demon," "Blood," "Yentl the Yeshiva Boy." Even Irving Howe, whose advocacy became inflected with concern that Singer risked getting "mired in his own originality," cast his criticism as a warning about the hazards of mastery: "Singer seems almost perfect within his stringent limits, but it is perfection of stasis." Howe's reservations were still those of a sympathetically inclined critic—he edited the Modern Library volume *Selected Short Stories of Isaac Bashevis Singer* in 1966—and for most American readers, Singer's performances as a storyteller were embraced as dazzling inventions. If the range of subject matter and style was somewhat restricted, as Howe maintained, Singer's "stringent limits" were more than compensated by his startling frankness, his seamless fusion of archaic and modern, and his willingness to entertain his readers in an era given to anxious ruminations about alienation and existential crises. The consistency in the tales posed little danger of wearying through monotony. On the contrary, these stories were more likely to deliver a bracing shock of the new. However easy it is to regard Singer as a magical realist *avant la lettre* from the vantage of the twenty-first century, the stories resembled little else on the American literary horizon when they were first published in English.

Singer began to reach new readers by placing stories in magazines that, scarcely a few years earlier, would have seemed well beyond the purview of a Yiddish writer in translation. Since the appearance of "Gimpel the Fool" in *Partisan Review*, his tales had been published in magazines aimed at a Jewish-American audience such as *Commentary* and the Zionist quarterly *Midstream*. Starting in the early 1960s, however, his stories were featured in *Mademoiselle*, *Esquire*, *GQ*, and *The Saturday Evening Post*; he was soon contributing to *Encounter* and *Harper's* and writing the occasional essay about Yiddish culture—the stories of Sholem Aleichem, the past glories of Second Avenue theater—for *The New York Times*. In 1967, he branched out even further, publishing three stories in *Playboy* and contributing "The Slaughterer" to *The New Yorker*, prompting the magazine to abandon a policy against publishing stories in translation. Singer's relationship with *The New Yorker*, the magazine that for American fiction writers was the *ne plus ultra* of literary prestige, was especially fruitful, as he developed a close professional rapport with editor Rachel MacKenzie, who worked on his stories with particular care and attention. Singer entered into an agreement whereby a story of his in English could be acquired by another magazine only if *The New Yorker* turned it down first. This wasn't often the case, as after the publication of "The Slaughterer," most of his stories made their debuts in English in the magazine.

By the time Singer became a regular *New Yorker* contributor his works had long been thriving in English, the result of years of his active involvement in preparing translations. "Gimpel the Fool" and other stories published in English during the 1950s had been translated without his direct participation. But Singer, aware of how Yiddish writers such as Sholem Aleichem had not been well served by their translators, was quite savvy about the benefits of authorized English translations in the United States and abroad—nearly all translations of his works into other languages were based on the English versions—and established a sort of translation workshop in his Upper West Side

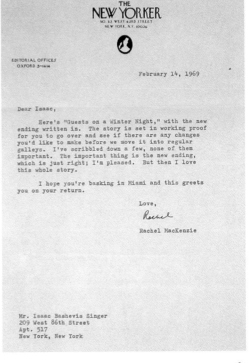

55. Letter to Singer dated February 24, 1969, from Rachel MacKenzie, Singer's editor at *The New Yorker*.

apartment, where he would meet with collaborators in daily sessions to prepare honed versions of his works in English. Excepting translators such as Joseph Singer (Israel Joshua's son), Mirra Ginsburg, and several others, the collaborators identified in the translation credits to his stories and novels often did not know Yiddish. "I dictate to them in English, my English," Singer described the process in 1975. "They polish my English." By the 1970s Singer was comfortable enough with his facility in the language of his adopted homeland to call English, in the introduction to his story collection *A Crown of Feathers* (1973), his "second original language"—though this phrase was not so much a comment on the degree of his fluency in English as a remark about his tendency to revise as he reconsidered his work. As all his bilingual readers and Singer himself conceded, much was lost in translation, but his efforts shaping his English translations gave them the authority of being parallel versions of his Yiddish texts, rather than merely diminished approximations of the originals.

Singer's reputation as master storyteller and, increasingly, gracious emissary of *Yiddishkeit* was enhanced by his visibility as the subject of interviews and feature stories in the American press. For Singer it was a happy accident of historical timing (one of the few) that his elevation as a celebrity author coincided with the rise of the interview as a vehicle of publicity. Fashioning his persona as a writer, he used the forum of the interview to great advantage. Its blend of informality and seriousness was well suited to his temperament and considerable personal charm, offering a format in which discussions of his stories and novels, his work habits, politics, literary influences, philosophy, spirituality, and Jewish tradition could be leavened with shrewd anecdotes, recollections of Poland before the Holocaust, and droll flashes of wit. Singer gave hundreds of interviews over the course of his career, on television and radio as well as in journals of sober intellectual comment, specialized quarterlies, literary "little magazines," modest local papers and national weeklies, and vivid glossies like *Vogue*, *Esquire*, and *Interview*. Given the relative paucity of his literary essays available in English, particularly in light of his voluminous output as a fiction writer and memoirist, such conversations were the primary channel by which he elaborated his personal philosophy in public. In lively exchanges with favorably disposed questioners, Singer ranged freely across his myriad interests, from the cosmic to the trivial, from the esoteric to the mundane. In 1975, the first published excerpts from Richard time to devote to it – but I'll manage somehow.

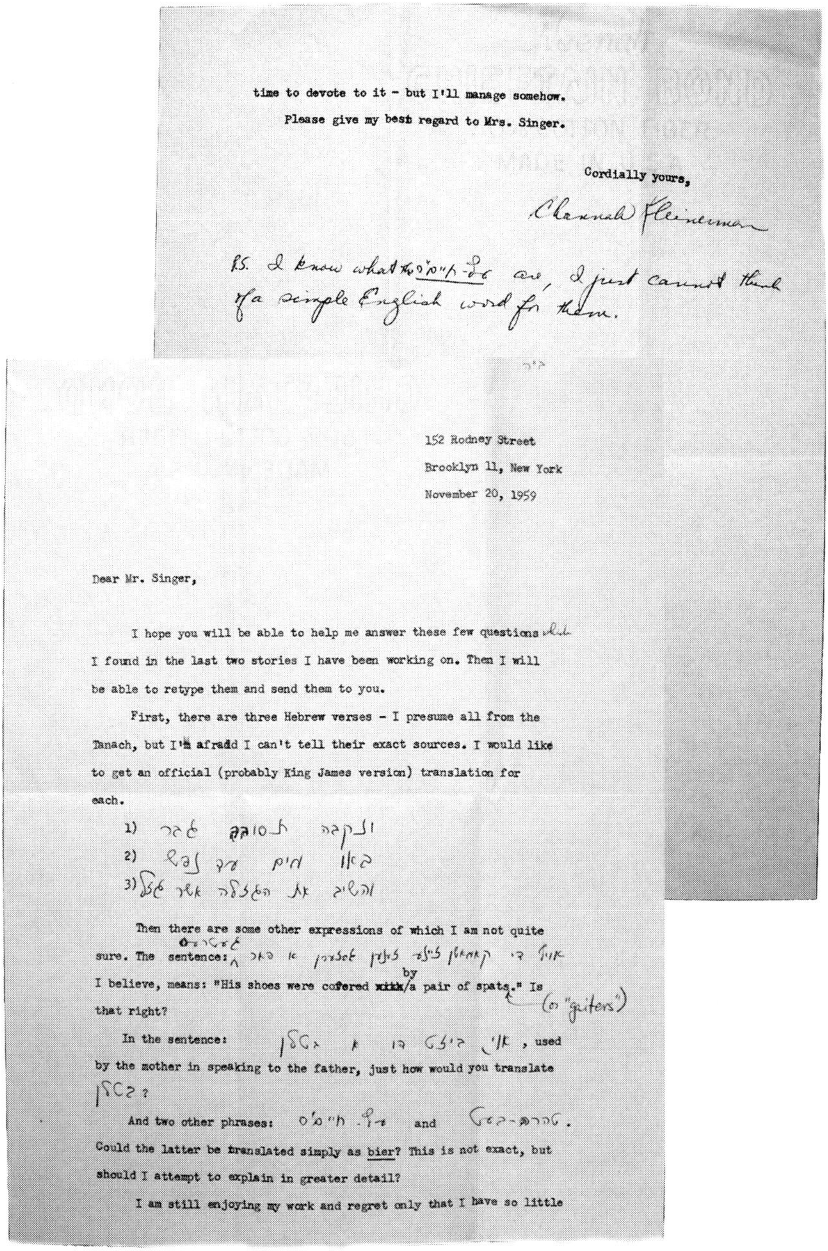

Please give my best regard to Mrs. Singer.

Cordially yours,

Channah Fleinerman

P.S. I know what ‏קיוסקערס‏ are, I just cannot think of a simple English word for them.

‏ב"ה‏

152 Rodney Street

Brooklyn 11, New York

November 20, 1959

Dear Mr. Singer,

I hope you will be able to help me answer these few questions which I found in the last two stories I have been working on. Then I will be able to retype them and send them to you.

First, there are three Hebrew verses – I presume all from the Tanach, but I'm afraid I can't tell their exact sources. I would like to get an official (probably King James version) translation for each.

1) ‏וַיִּשְׁמַע שָׁלוֹם עָלֶיךָ‏

2) ‏בָּאִי עִם מַה זָּה לָךְ‏

3) ‏וַיֹּאמֶר אֵלָיו הֲשָׁלוֹם אֵלָיו נָחֹרְ‏

Then there are some other expressions of which I am not quite sure. The sentence: ‏זוֹג מִנְּעָלָיו הָיוּ מְכֻסִּים בְּזוּג קַלּוֹשֶׁן‏ I believe, means: "His shoes were covered with/a pair of spats." Is that right? (or "guiters")

In the sentence: ‏אֵיךְ סְבָרָה זוֹ אָ סַוְדֶן‏ , used by the mother in speaking to the father, just how would you translate ‏סַוְדֶן‏ ?

And two other phrases: ‏פֶּרֶק חַיִּים‏ and ‏פַּרְנֶעסְל‏ . Could the latter be translated simply as bier? This is not exact, but should I attempt to explain in greater detail?

I am still enjoying my work and regret only that I have so little

Burgin's extensive discussions with Singer spanning some fifty hours of talk, eventually boiled down and edited as the book *Conversations with Isaac Bashevis Singer* (1986), was given the title: "Isaac Bashevis Singer Talks . . . About Everything."

Or not quite everything. Much of Singer's appeal was based on a sense of his accessibility. Despite his gifts, he did not come across as aloof or self-important; until he won the Nobel Prize in 1978, his name was listed in the phone book. "I write between one phone call and another," he told the *Washington Post* in

57. Singer at his typewriter.

1976. His habits had become well known: he was a vegetarian, he liked long walks, he was fond of taking meals in cafeterias like the Famous Dairy Restaurant just off Broadway on West 72nd Street. As reflected in the subtitle of Paul Kresh's admiring biography, *The Magician of West 86th Street*, Singer came to be regarded as a kind of beneficent spirit of Manhattan's Upper West Side, a neighborhood known for its refugees who had fled or survived Hitler's onslaught. Nevertheless, Singer was not without his secrets, and his openness toward the audiences at his

lectures and the readers who sought him out was joined with a curious sort of public reticence, as if he were hiding in plain sight. His many memoirs did not extend the narrative of his life past his first lean years in the United States. His more recent past could perhaps be glimpsed—but if so, obscurely—in the many stories featuring a nameless writer traveling abroad, in Brazil or Argentina, Portugal or Israel, or in tales in which a stranger contacts a renowned Yiddish author to unburden himself (frequently, herself) of a story.

These works, however, tend to undermine their ostensibly autobiographical basis by unfolding more like fiction than real life. There are improbable coincidences, dramatic reversals of fortune, and dreamlike epiphanies. "Brother Beetle," for example, first published in the *Forward* in 1965, is narrated by a Polish-born Jewish writer now living in the United States who is making a visit to Israel. The story's narrator seems identical with Singer, as though the episode were a page from his autobiography; toward the end of the story, he even reveals the address of his childhood home in Warsaw as 10 Krochmalna Street. Its central incident, however, is indebted to melodrama, even bedroom farce, though the mood is fraught with tension: a tryst is interrupted by the intrusion of the woman's jealous lover, and the writer finds himself naked, shivering, crouching "like an animal at bay waiting for the hunter to shoot" on the roof of her apartment building (not suspecting trouble, he had simply gone out to use the bathroom). The theatricality of the situation suggests that Singer has inserted himself as a character in a black-comic fantasy of his own devising, blurring the line between fact and artifice, storytelling and autobiography.

For some, however, a story like "Brother Beetle" might have seemed less a brilliant exploration of the porous border between truth and fiction than evidence of adulterous proclivities. Rumored accusations that usually took the form of loose talk and gossip sometimes found their way into print. While in Jerusalem to accept an honorary degree from Hebrew University in 1975, he was assailed in an unflattering article published in the *Jerusalem Post* by his nephew Maurice Carr, who recalled Singer being "an escape artist, the sex-Houdini" back in Warsaw and claimed he had visited a "cherished mistress" while in Israel six years earlier. Among Yiddish writers, mutterings about what were perceived as Singer's personal failings fed into a larger resentment about his meteoric rise to success in translation.

58. Singer in his West 86th Street apartment.

Cynthia Ozick's novella "Envy; or, Yiddish in America," first published in *Commentary* in November 1969 and included in her story collection *The Pagan Rabbi*, gives a sense of the bilious rage caused by Singer's fame in Yiddish literary circles. The poet Edelshtein—perhaps based on Jacob Glatstein, one of Singer's fiercest critics—and his friend Baumzweig shared an "agreed hatred for the man they called *der chazer*. He was named Pig because of his extraordinarily white skin, like a tissue of pale ham, and also because he had become unbelievably famous. When they did not call him Pig they called him *shed*—Devil. They also called him Yankee Doodle. His name was Yankel Ostrover, and he was a writer of stories." Through the distorting filter of Edelshtein's spleen, a caricature of Singer emerges. Ostover writes about "insanely sexual, pornographic, paranoid, freakish" subjects; his "impure" Yiddish sentences "lacked grace and sweep"; he had risen from a hack "squeezer-out of real-life tales" for the Yiddish press to a celebrity commanding hefty lecture fees because he "sleeps with the right translators."

Now in his sixties, professionally secure, and living quite comfortably, Singer could easily shrug off such resentment. In addition to his prolific writing of stories and novels—*Enemies, A Love Story* had been serialized in the *Forward* in 1966, followed the next year by *The Certificate*—he embraced yet another literary genre and began composing children's stories. Responding to a request by his friend and translator Elizabeth Shub, Singer wrote his first stories for children in the mid-1960s. After a failed initial effort, Singer created "Zlateh the Goat," a moving fable commemorating Hanukkah. A young boy named Aaron, unhappily following his father's orders to deliver a goat to be slaughtered for the Hanukkah feast, is caught in a snowstorm and survives the ordeal with help from the animal, who nourishes him with her milk. The story was collected with six other children's tales in *Zlateh the Goat and Other Stories*, published by Harper & Row in 1966; the book included pictures by Maurice Sendak, an admirer of Singer's fiction who offered to contribute illustrations when he spied the manuscript on the desk of an editor at Harper & Row. *Zlateh the Goat* inaugurated a new phase of Singer's career in which writing for children figured prominently. Between 1966 and 1976, he published fourteen books for young readers, collaborating with artists such as Antonio Frasconi, Margot Zemach, and the photographer Roman Vishniac. A generation of children grew up reading and being read to from books such as *When Shlemiel Went to Warsaw* and *Naftali the Storyteller and His Horse, Sus.*

While it's not unusual for a popular and beloved writer to try writing for children, Singer came to regard his children's stories as far more substantial than a mere adjunct to his "adult" fiction. His stories for young readers—many of whom, it turned out, weren't so young after all—differ from his other fiction primarily in the muting of his sense of irony, the unavoidable conventions of tone and vocabulary specific to a juvenile readership, and, not surprisingly, a less explicit treatment of violence and eroticism, though in the children's stories these trademark Singer concerns are not abandoned but are transposed into a different key. He claimed that tales meant for children imply an ideal relationship between writer and audience, because unlike modern adults, whose heads have been filled with fashionable cant about

59. The cover of Singer's first book of tales for children, *Zlateh the Goat and Other Stories*, with illustrations by Maurice Sendak., published by Harper & Row in 1966. The collection received a Newberry Award. Sendak was delighted to collaborate on the project; a postcard in the Harry Ransom Center's collection of Singer's papers sends warm regards: "Dear Mr. Singer: Did not want to wait till Monday to tell you how much I enjoyed the new stories! Wonderful, wonderful— I can't wait to draw fat Jewish servants disguised as angels!" Sendak once wryly remarked that his "father and mother *finally* became impressed by their youngest child when he teamed up with Isaac Bashevis Singer."

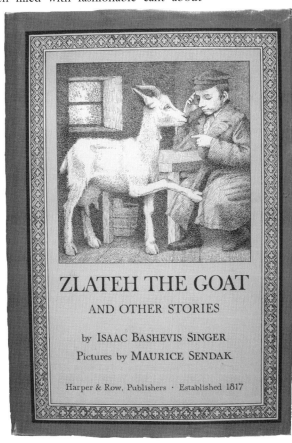

ZLATEH THE GOAT

AND OTHER STORIES

by ISAAC BASHEVIS SINGER

Pictures by MAURICE SENDAK

Harper & Row, Publishers · Established 1817

politics, sociology, and psychology, the child still experiences the tension and resolution of a well-crafted story as an immediate, unique, incomparable experience. In an essay published in *The New York Times* in November 1969, "I See the Child as a Last Refuge," Singer reflected on his enthusiasm for children's fiction as a means of delivering a sweeping rejection of twentieth-century literature. "No writer can bribe his way to the child's attention with false originality, literary puns and puzzles, arbitrary distortions of the order of things, or muddy streams of consciousness which often reveal nothing but a writer's boring and selfish personality. I came to the child because I see in him a last refuge from a literature gone berserk and ready for suicide."

The adversarial posture was hardly new: since his Warsaw days Singer had regarded himself, rightly, as an anomaly among Yiddish writers and derided most of his contemporaries, particularly those seduced by communism. In his later years, his maverick stance was imbued with an increasingly strident conservatism. The enchanting qualities of the children's stories—the gentle yet never saccharine narration, the sly humor, the overriding sense of awe at the world's mysteries—are at odds with the certainties of an essay like "I See the Child as a Last Refuge." And though he chastised twentieth-century writers for eschewing their craft as storytellers in favor of "writing essays about their heroes" (a judgment curiously blind to the way ideas inform many of his best novels and stories, such as *Shadows on the Hudson* and "The Cafeteria"), Singer himself used his fiction as a pulpit for a screed against contemporary ills. *Der bal-tshuve* (*The Penitent*), a novel serialized in the *Forward* in 1973 and published in English ten years later, is as tendentious as any of the books that Singer claimed had set literature on the road to destruction. Except for a short prefatory chapter, the book is a monologue delivered by an Orthodox Jew named Joseph Shapiro, who despises secularism in all its forms; America, the kibbutz, and above all sexually liberated women are singled out for attack. *The Penitent* presents a wholesale repudiation of "modern man": "One of modern man's most inane passions is reading newspapers in order to keep up with the latest news. The news is always bad and it poisons your life, but modern man can't live without this poison. He must know about all the murders, all the rapes. He must know about all the insanities and false theories." *The Penitent*'s Joseph Shapiro brings forth a blanket indictment, a renunciation of virtually everything outside

60. Singer in 1986 with Dvorah Menashe (later Telushkin), who met him at Bard College in 1975 and became his secretary, translator, and a close companion. Her memoir *Master of Dreams* is an account of their relationship.

of Orthodox Judaism. When it was published in English, it included an author's note—indeed, a short "essay about his hero"—clarifying the difference between Singer's philosophy and his protagonist's: "The agonies and the disenchantment of Joseph Shapiro may to a degree stir a self-evaluation in both believers and skeptics. The remedies that he recommends may not heal everybody's wounds, but the nature of the sickness will, I hope, be recognized."

Singer's jeremiad in *The Penitent*, even if ventriloquized through a character whose embrace of Orthodoxy as a cure for the modern "sickness" was not one Singer could adopt himself, derived from a sense of the authority of his pronouncements, now that he had long been the most famous Yiddish writer

61. Singer in the courtyard of the Belnord apartment building at 225 West 86th Street, where he and Alma lived in the 1960s, 1970s, and 1980s.

alive. If *The Penitent* expressed a profound quarrel with the world, its criticisms seemed belied by Singer's cosmopolitan enjoyment of his fame. There was, as well, the simple fact of his prosperity, which fit the myth of the immigrant success story for those inclined to see it that way: four decades after his arrival at Ellis Island, after impoverished beginnings in America and years of hard work, Singer was now an affluent Manhattanite who lived in a tony apartment building—the Belnord, on West 86th Street—and had recently bought a second home in a Miami Beach condominium. And the accolades kept coming. The film *Mrs. Pupko's Beard and Isaac Singer's Dream*, photographer and filmmaker Bruce Davidson's free adaptation of Singer's story "The Beard," was featured on PBS's "American Masters" series in December 1972, paired with a documentary about Marc Chagall. In 1974, the year after writing *The Penitent*, he received the National Book Award for his story collection *A Crown of Feathers* (sharing the prize with Thomas Pynchon for *Gravity's Rainbow*). A stage adaptation of "Yentl the Yeshiva Boy" premiered to enthusiastic reviews; it soon moved to Broadway, where it enjoyed a successful five-month run followed by a national tour. Film rights had been acquired for several of his novels and stories. He was a household name in America, and for well over a decade critics had mentioned Singer as deserving the Nobel Prize in Literature. When the call came in November 1978 that the Swedish Academy had selected him for its highest honor, it marked the final stage of Singer's unlikely apotheosis as an exemplar of Jewish culture, the last great Yiddish writer—perhaps the last Yiddish writer, period—in the eyes of the world.

62. Architectural detail above the courtyard entrance of the Belnord.

Francine Prose: When I first began teaching college undergraduates and MFA students in the early 1980s, I used to assign Isaac Bashevis Singer's "A Crown of Feathers" as a model of pure storytelling, an example of how complex and dazzling an apparently straightforward narrative could be. I enjoyed introducing my students to a masterpiece so dense with incident and detail, propelled by startling reverses, plot twists and turns, improbable events that took on an equally unlikely verisimilitude thanks to the acuity of the author's understanding of human nature and the depth of his inquiry into our fierce, unsettled relationship with the metaphysical. Just a few days ago, the latest edition of the same short-story anthology from which I used to teach arrived in the mail, and I was surprised and appalled to see that "A Crown of Feathers" had been excised—exorcised, you might say—from the collection. On rereading the story, after many years, I thought I understood why. I found it no less beautiful, but far more extreme than I recalled, more shocking in its eroticism, its strangeness, its willingness to follow the threads of narrative wherever they might lead, and in its insistence on looking beneath the surface pieties of religion to examine the unruly hungers, obsessions, rages, griefs, and mysteries that faith and culture address. On rereading "A Crown of Feathers," I felt as if time had been polishing the story in my absence. It seemed brighter than I remembered, more subversive, more like a beacon of harsh, peculiar truth to guide us through a time in which, even as the world around us grows steadily more sectarian and brutal, we are encouraged to pretend that one purpose of literature is to lie about sex and religion, to argue that eroticism and faith are forces that, in every case, make us more tolerant and rational, more loving, patient, and kind.

63. Singer signing copies of his short-story collection *A Crown of Feathers* (1973).

Harvey Shapiro:

It was at the Jewish Workmen's Circle in Lower Manhattan, in the fall of 1966, that I got my first glimpse of Isaac Bashevis Singer. I had gone there to hear a discussion of Jewish-American literature—discussions there were usually in Yiddish but that night's was to be in English—and partly out of loyalty to my friend Harvey Swados, who along with Irving Howe and Singer was to speak. The place was packed when I got there but I managed to find a seat next to Jean Garrigue (for me, *the* Village poet in those days) and her lover, the novelist Josephine Herbst. In any case, what I remember of the evening's proceedings concerns only Singer.

When his turn came, he spoke with great conviction of the need to maintain contact with one's Jewish roots, whether one was a doctor, lawyer, writer, whatever, in order to achieve anything in this world. At the end of the talks there was to be a question period; I had been warned that questions at the Jewish Workmen's Circle often became speeches. A middle-aged gentleman rose first and addressed

64. Singer lecturing at the University of Miami in 1979.

his question to Mr. Singer. He had a nephew, a brilliant boy now at Harvard, who had never gone to *cheder* and, in fact, had never shown any interest in his cultural heritage. But his nephew, he was convinced, could be a Supreme Court justice, maybe even another Felix Frankfurter. Would Mr. Singer deny him this possibility just because he wasn't interested in things Jewish? And then he went into a ten-minute recitation of his nephew's sterling qualities.

Finally, he was through. Singer stepped forward and said: "I have a niece."

Singer entered American literature with the publication of his story "Gimpel the Fool," translated by Saul Bellow, in *Partisan Review*. How that translation was done was told to me by the Yiddish poet Eliezer Greenberg, "Lazer" to his friends. It was in his flat, he said. He, standing, read the Yiddish text and Bellow, at the typewriter, typed the English words. It was done in one sitting. Bellow offered to do more stories but Singer—fearful, I suppose, of becoming part of Bellow's oeuvre—said, no, thanks.

65. A letter from one of Singer's young readers.

Beth David
7500 S.W. 120th St.
Miami, Fla. 33183
11/13/78

Dear Mr. Singer,

Our teacher read some of your stories to us. She read Shlemiel Goes to Warsaw, Three Wishes, Shrewd Todie And Lyzer the Mizer and Shlemiel the, Businessman. I Like Shlemiel the, Businessman Because he always had the wrong goat at the right time, then the right goat at the wrong time.

Yours truly,
Jay Rudolph

The Prize

1978

SINGER flew to Sweden in December 1978 to accept the Nobel Prize at the annual ceremony held in Stockholm. He traveled with a small entourage that included Alma, *Forward* editor Simon Weber, his longtime editor Robert Giroux, and his publisher Roger Straus and his wife, Dorothea, who had helped translate many stories in the late 1960s and 1970s. Israel Zamir joined the celebration and covered the event for the Tel Aviv newspaper *Al ha-Mishmar*. On December 10, along with eight laureates from other fields, Singer was presented the award by Swedish King Carl XVI Gustaf. Accepting the prize, he quipped that he wrote for children because "children read books, not reviews," and told the gala assembly of some 1,200 guests that he liked to write ghost stories—"and nothing fits a ghost better than a dying language." The five other laureates from America were honored with renditions of Gershwin's "Of Thee I Sing"; emphasizing his immigration, the orchestra honored Singer by playing the intermezzo from Swedish composer Hilding Rosenberg's 1932 opera "Journey to America."

66. Singer and Alma with Roger Straus at the National Arts Club in New York City during the late 1970s.

Two days earlier, Singer had delivered his Nobel Prize Lecture on Literature, a twenty-minute speech that touched on familiar themes of his personal credo: the belief that the writer

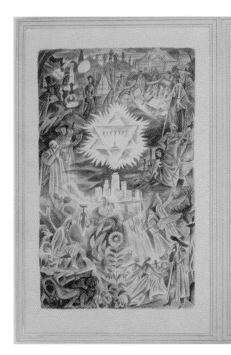

must be "an entertainer of the spirit," a grim evaluation of contemporary history, and a faith in the messianic power of creativity ("the pessimism of the creative person is not decadence but a mighty passion for the redemption of man"). Most of the lecture, however, is a paean to Yiddish. "The truth is what the great religions preached, the Yiddish-speaking people of the ghettos practiced day in and day out." In the middle of the speech, which was delivered in English, Singer interjected a sentence in Yiddish, a language he was all but certain had never resounded in the halls of the Swedish Academy. He went on to praise the "Yiddish spirit" for its "pious joy, lust for life, longing for the Messiah, patience and deep appreciation of human individuality." Even now, the language "contains treasures that have not been revealed to the eyes of the world."

The affirmation of Yiddish language and culture in Singer's Nobel lecture marked the endpoint of a long trajectory. First there was the budding young writer who had learned modern Hebrew and considered abandoning Yiddish altogether. Later, in his first years in the United States, Singer was troubled by the intrusion of Americanisms into Yiddish and what he regarded as the language's difficulties in representing the modern world. In

67. Certificate for the Nobel Prize in Literature presented to Singer in 1978 by the Swedish Academy of Arts and Letters, lauding Singer's "impassioned narrative art which, with roots in a Polish-Jewish cultural tradition, brings the universal human condition to life."

the 1940s he despaired that Yiddish literature had become stuck in the impasse of being "godly without a god, worldly without a world." Only well after the war, in which the vast majority of the world's Yiddish speakers had been murdered, was Singer able to make celebratory remarks such as Yiddish "has vitamins other languages haven't got" or, as he wrote in the concluding sentence of his Nobel lecture, "In a figurative way Yiddish is the wise and humble language of us all, the idiom of frightened and hopeful humanity."

Singer's invocation of a "figurative" sense of Yiddish as a language belonging to everyone was a reflection of the award's humanist underpinnings (writing on behalf of the Nobel Committee, the Swedish Academy of Letters praised Singer for bringing "the universal human condition to life"). Yet it also pointed up the decline of Yiddish: anyone might lay claim to its "idiom" in a generalized fashion, but the number of people actually speaking and writing the language was rapidly dwindling. In Israel, Jews grew up speaking Hebrew. Elsewhere English, Spanish, and other languages had supplanted Yiddish as the mother tongue. He told the assembled dignitaries in Stockholm that "Yiddish has not said its last word," but his hopefulness derived from the futility of making predictions about the future, since even with languages unforeseeable outcomes do occur: the near-miraculous resuscitation of Hebrew in the twentieth century was a case in point. But in Singer's address there were no younger Yiddish writers mentioned, no recent Yiddish literary renaissance to point to.

As a literary judgment, the Nobel Prize crowned Singer's long career with an honor no Yiddish writer had ever received, not Sholem Asch, not his brother Israel Joshua, not even I. L. Peretz, the towering patriarch of Yiddish letters. As a commemoration of Yiddish, the award carried a more melancholy burden of belatedly recognizing a language and tradition whose survival was by no means certain. Singer was aware that his single sentence of Yiddish spoken in the assembly hall of the Swedish Academy was the first and last words of his native language that would ever be uttered there. As an occasion to reflect upon a writer and his language, the ceremonies in Stockholm fused Singer's personal triumph with a plaintive sense that one of the world's great literary traditions was in the midst of passing away.

68. New York City street signs at Broadway and West 86th Street, which was given the ceremonial name "Isaac Bashevis Singer Boulevard" along a stretch of the street near the Belnord on the Upper West Side.

69. Singer behind the Surfside Towers, the condominium where he lived in Florida,
February 13, 1986.

"It Always Had To Do With His Writing"

1979–1991

IN later years Singer spent much of his time at his second home in Surfside, Florida, on the northern end of Miami Beach, living in the condominium apartment he had purchased in 1973. He had grown fond of Miami Beach as a place to work during extended winter visits with Alma in the late 1940s and 1950s. Reminiscing late in life about these first trips to Florida, he recalled how Miami Beach had been "a hub of Jewishness" and "a continuation of the little town" in which he "saw again a piece of home." He heard familiar jokes that had survived the transatlantic crossing intact. The varied Yiddish dialects spoken in cafeterias and hotel lobbies revealed precise origins in specific Polish villages. "The sound of the Old World," he mused, "was as alive as ever."

Singer set four stories and a sizeable chunk of *Shadows on the Hudson* in Miami Beach. As is so often the case, his fiction suggests more complex feelings about the place than those expressed in remarks made at the end of his life. With its tropical climate, gaudily colored buildings, luxury shops, and bikini-clad bathers, Miami Beach was the antithesis of Singer's origins in the cramped apartment on Krochmalna Street, that "stronghold of Jewish puritanism, where the body was looked upon as a mere appendage to the soul." Although he enjoyed Florida, Singer usually characterized Miami Beach in his fiction as a profoundly alien place, an extreme manifestation of the America he believed was unable to sustain more enduring values than commerce and mindless leisure. One character in *Shadows on the Hudson* observes that "here no one feared evil spirits. . . . Here hedonism was already an established religion." In one of his first stories to take place in the United States, "Alone," a nameless visitor to Miami Beach, mysteriously evicted from his hotel, drifts aimlessly and imagines having survived a disaster of Biblical proportions: "Mankind, it seemed, had perished in some catastrophe, and I was left, like Noah—but in an empty ark, without sons, without a wife, without any animals." In "Old Love," a suicide in a Miami Beach condominium much like Singer's own elicits the lament, "People lose their minds in

70. Singer and Alma, February 13, 1986, Surfside, Florida.

71. Singer and Alma at a Surfside cafeteria, October 1989.

America." Even his most affectionate depiction of the beachfront community, "A Party in Miami Beach," is tinged with satire.

As one might expect, after Singer won the Nobel Prize he remained in the public eye. The publication of his *Collected Stories* in 1982 was an occasion for critics and readers to take the measure of his achievement as a storyteller. Late the next year, *Yentl*, Barbra Streisand's film of "Yentl the Yeshiva Boy," opened in movie theaters nationwide. Starring Amy Irving, Mandy Patinkin, and Streisand herself in the lead role, *Yentl* was neither the first nor last cinematic adaptation of Singer's work—an Israeli production of *The Magician of Lublin* had been screened at film festivals and had a limited run in New York in 1978, and Paul Mazursky's film of *Enemies, A Love Story* was released in 1989. But *Yentl* was by far the most lavish and com-

mercially successful. It was met with mixed reviews, as critics acknowledged the film's shortcomings but for the most part approved the sentiment on display, applauding its "earnestness" and "heartfelt" sincerity. The movie's harshest detractor was Isaac Bashevis Singer. Taking the form of an interview with himself, his grievances with *Yentl* were published in *The New York Times* in January 1984. "I must say that Miss Streisand was exceedingly kind to herself," Singer wrote. "The result is that Miss Streisand is always present, while poor Yentl is absent." He objected especially to the transformation

72. Movie poster for Barbra Streisand's *Yentl* (1983).

73. Singer and Alma on 95th Street in Surfside, near their condominium, the Surfside Towers. The street was given the ceremonial name "Isaac Singer Boulevard."

of the story into a musical, and a new ending that has Yentl traveling to America: "This kitsch ending summarizes all the faults of the adaptation. It was done without any kinship to Yentl's character, her ideals, her sacrifice, her great passion for spiritual achievement. As it is, the whole splashy production has nothing but commercial value."

Although his output of new works dwindled almost to nothing as he entered his ninth decade, Singer continued to put together collections of stories in English drawn from his reserve of Yiddish stories: *The Image* was published in 1985, followed by *The Death of Methuselah* in 1988. Sadly, his final years were marked by failing health and mental incapacity, apparently brought on by Alzheimer's. "He was just not there," recalled Dorothea Straus to Singer's biographer Janet Hadda. "Once in a while he would come back and he would say things like, 'I certainly am the greatest Yiddish writer living.' He would be out of it completely, like a child, and then he would come back. And suddenly he was his old self. But it always had to do with his writing." On July 24, 1991, Isaac Singer died at his home in Surfside, Florida.

74. Singer
in Florida,
October 1986.

75. Singer amid the clutter of his apartment in Manhattan, May 23, 1987.

76. Singer and his typewriter in his Surfside apartment, February 12, 1986.

The Achievement of Isaac Bashevis Singer
A Roundtable Discussion

The following is an edited transcript of a discussion dedicated to Singer's life and works moderated by Max Rudin, publisher of The Library of America. Participants included Morris Dickstein, Jonathan Rosen, David Roskies, Isaiah Sheffer, and Ilan Stavans.

MAX RUDIN: When Isaac Bashevis Singer was awarded the Nobel Prize, he wrote to the Swedish Academy, "It's a wonderful surprise, not only for me, but for all Yiddish readers. They feel rightly this honor was given to them, too, because of their faithfulness to their roots and to their culture." And in some respects Singer emerges from the Nobel Prize period as representative and spokesman for Eastern European Yiddish culture. Is that fair? Is that a good way to understand the place of his work in literature?

MORRIS DICKSTEIN: I think it's unusual for him to be representative. And it's interesting that he says he accepts it as an honor to Yiddish readers and not to Yiddish writers, since he had contempt for most other Jewish and Yiddish writers. And mostly he had contempt for the whole Yiddish literary tradition. He saw himself as reaching back to earlier Jewish traditions and away from Yiddish traditions that he saw as polluted by socialism and sentimentality. Also, this is late Singer, and kind of an official moment. I think earlier he rarely saw himself as representative of anything.

ILAN STAVANS: It is interesting that he says Yiddish readers, too, in that he's not representing American Yiddish readers. I was thinking of this answer more in the context of the ethnic writer that Singer has become in the United States in representing the American Jews. To some extent the ethnic writer always is pushed to represent African-American readers, or Latino readers, or Asian-American readers.

DAVID ROSKIES: Well, the first thing I would say is that roots and culture are wonderful buzzwords, and they're unexceptionable. And that's what I think he does to position himself as an All-American writer. I mean, really, who would take exception to a writer who speaks in the name of roots and culture? That's like motherhood and apple pie. But you're right—it's balanced by the fact that it's Yiddish. But Yiddish is fuzzy and warm, just like roots and culture are fuzzy and warm. So I guess I would use that as the foil for the Singer who was anything but fuzzy and warm.

I think his strength as a writer from beginning to end was in opposition to a very distinct culture and cultural tradition. It's true that he was at war with socialism and humanism. One of the great turning points in his life was coming to America in 1935. And the writer's block that he suffered—seven years, basically, where he completely dries up as a writer. Because he discovers the demise of Yiddish as a living language in this country. And what is he going to do? He has this linguistic medium. It's what he knows best. And the readers—these same loyal readers have abandoned him, have betrayed him. They're speaking a *patois*, a pidgin Yiddish, beneath contempt. No self-respecting writer could write the language that is spoken in the streets of New York and Miami Beach. So what is a writer to do?

In his own brilliant dialectical way, he decides that the answer, at least for the time being, is to renounce the American present, renounce his readers, renounce the degraded

77. Doodles
by Singer.

state of Jewish culture in America, and go back to some re-imagined past. To me that's the root of his greatness from beginning to end.

JONATHAN ROSEN: He is redefining what Yiddish literature is. Now it is synonymous with him. He may have started out writing in opposition to the tradition, but that's the nature of tragic Jewish history. He started out as the first of the Mohicans, and now he's the last of the Mohicans because the world changed around him. And so he now knows that people will identify him with Yiddish literature, even if they're not reading him in Yiddish.

I worked at the *Forward* when it had become the emblem of what a Jewish newspaper was supposed to be. Nobody spoke about all the Yiddish newspapers it had argued with and quarreled with. And that context is the thing that made the *Forward* alive and meaningful. So it's kind of the blessing and the curse of being last or one of the last.

MORRIS DICKSTEIN: It's possible to be so traditional that you're radical. It's true that he did become more reactionary toward the end of his life. In books like *The Penitent* and so on he sort of presented himself as someone who scorned much of the modern world. On the other hand, by reaching

back from immediate traditions to earlier traditions he showed that a use could be made of them that made them seem radical and even modern within a contemporary literary context.

MAX RUDIN: Let's talk briefly about Singer's use of the supernatural.

JONATHAN ROSEN: His father was a mystically inclined rabbi, who literally predicted the Messiah would come on a certain date. His brother tells a story in his memoir about rocking the cradle that Isaac was lying in and getting so excited hearing his father talk about how the Messiah was about to come that Isaac actually flew out of the cradle.

And his maternal grandfather was a rationalist rabbi. This was a conversation inside Judaism, which is both a natural and a supernatural religion. Singer is roughly contemporaneous with Gershom Scholem, who was suddenly telling people that this seemingly hidden occult stream of Judaism is actually as large and formative as the seemingly normative tradition above it. Partly Singer was doing what writers always do, which is just drawing on his inheritance, on his background.

78. Three self-portrait doodles by Singer.

ISAIAH SHEFFER: I can tell you one practical anecdote that might shed light on it. I was working with him on the adaptation

96

of his "Shlemiel" stories into a play. And at one point, the plot requires that Shlemiel be turned around and head back to the same town that he's just left. And we were sitting in his living room on 86th Street thinking, how does the guy get turned around? We were trying to find a plot device for this folktale. And at one point, I swear to you, he said, "Listen, maybe a demon comes . . . Nah, nah." [*laughter*] And then we decided that a rascal turns his shoes around and points them back toward the other town. I think that's just a lightweight illustration that maybe his belief in the supernatural was something that he used as a literary tool.

MORRIS DICKSTEIN: Think of the Yeats line where the spirit comes to him and says, "I come to give you metaphors for poetry." In a way this is true for Singer as well. When he was growing up there he was someone who was very much involved in a world of ideas in Warsaw and elsewhere. The hot philosophy was rumors of Freud, Schopenhauer, Nietzsche. In other words, that element of modern culture, which is sort of the rediscovery of the irrational. And Singer had in his background—in his world—a fund of explanations that were very vividly dramatic explanations of the irrational.

He then proceeded to live life in a century where the irrational seemed to be dominating modern history. And so, he had something that he either did or did not believe in, but obviously believed in at some level as a way of explaining the paradoxes, and the cruelties, and the violence, and the motivations of human life as they were—then even more so—writ large in the contemporary history that threw him and his people from one place to another, and destroyed many of them and subjected them to things that he felt he had a way of explaining—or at least of dramatizing—this material, using it.

DAVID ROSKIES: I would call what Singer does not magic realism but demonic realism. And I think that he already perfected that in the old country. I think it's in *Satan in Goray* that he really shows his stuff. And what's new when he comes to America— and I maintain that 1943 is really the *annus mirabilis* of his career, that's when he really bursts forth as a genius after this prolonged silence. Two things are new. First of all, he returns to a very traditional form of Yiddish writing, I would say, the most traditional form—namely, the monologue, which was already passé. But all of modern Yiddish literature begins with the monologue out of the recognition that this is a spoken language, and the real strength of it is its spoken-ness. Sholem Aleichem, and Mendele Mocher Sforim, and Peretz—they perfected the monologue.

So, what happens in 1943 is Singer returns to this very old-fashioned literary form, and he perfects it on many grounds simultaneously. So he creates these magnificent monologists. Gimpel the Fool, the woman speaker in a story called "The Wife Killer." He creates a whole series of monologues. And, of course, those with the devil, his major mouthpiece.

But where he discovered this the first time was at the second ending of *Satan in Goray*, which is very modernist. He ends the novel twice. He has a realistic ending, and then he has a storybook ending. And the literary presence that runs away with the book is a dybbuk. He creates this dybbuk who starts blaspheming, and ripping apart the whole plot and the veneer of civility, and gives the story a completely different read, which has nothing to do with everything that we have understood to be the novel. It's really quite brilliant.

Okay, so now we flash forward, and it's 1943, and he gives the devil his due by making him the master storyteller. So, on the one hand, we're on familiar ground. We hear a voice. A highly articulate, Judaically knowledgeable, brilliantly idiomatic voice telling the story—only it's the devil. And it's the devil incarnate.

Where I think the real modernism and the genius of it is, is that it's narrated by the id. The devil becomes the spokesperson and the driving force of the id, who then proceeds to enter into the consciousness—the minds of each one of his victims—and adopts the voice and the sensibility, and the reading material of each one of his victims in turn. He is dramatizing the id, the force of evil, the demonic within each one of us in a way that it's never been done before.

ILAN STAVANS: I think as we analyze and as we discuss Singer transforming himself from a Yiddish Polish writer to an American writer, we need also to understand how the readership is changing. The readership that has been with him when he's writing *Satan in Goray* is very different from the

continued on page 100

Joyce Carol Oates: Storyteller, fabulist, prophet, and visionary, Isaac Bashevis Singer was long a master of what has become known in more recent decades as Magical Realism. His unique prose fiction defies easy classification, as the musical tone of his seemingly plain language eludes imitation. And how are we to understand his characters who are demonic, possessed, fated, resigned to their lot in a way utterly foreign to the "upbeat" spirit of America? *The way the dead eat, that's how they look* ("The Dead Fiddler") is a proverb out of a vanished world to which Isaac Singer had the key.

That Singer wrote his marvelous stories and novels in Yiddish, and supervised translations into English, is appropriate to the nature of his work: "I like to write ghost stories and nothing fits a ghost story better than a dying language. The deader the language, the more alive the ghost."

My favorite Singer stories are "ghostly" yet achingly "real." Such classics as "Gimpel the Fool" ("No doubt the world is entirely an imaginary world, but it is only once removed from the true world"); "The Spinoza of Market Street" with its unexpected, startling ending ("Divine Spinoza, forgive me. I have become a fool"); "Henne Fire" with its dazzle of outrageous passion, both erotic and spiritual ("Was it [Henne Fire's] fault that there was always a blaze within her?"). Possessing a very different sort of authority are Singer's American-set stories that are matter-of-factly narrated in the first person, as if the author were confiding in us: the blackly comic "The Lecture" ("My years in America seemed to have been swept away by [so much tragedy] and I was taken back, as though by magic, to my worst days in Poland"); "The Séance" ("There is no death, there isn't any. We live forever, and we love forever. This is the pure truth"); "The Cafeteria" ("If time and space are nothing more than forms of perception, as Kant argues, why shouldn't Hitler confer with his Nazis in a cafeteria on Broadway?").

Singer casts a spell. Open one of his books anywhere, the words leap out with a power that would seem to us demonic if it were not, at the very same time, so utterly plausible.

readership—the American Yiddish readership—that he encounters the first seven years. And then that readership transforms itself anew.

There's one moment in which he is having a radio conversation with Irving Howe, I believe it's at Princeton or at Yale. Later on it's transcribed in a *Midstream* text, where Singer actually tells Howe that he—Howe—is much more of a Yiddishist, of a Yiddish writer, than Singer himself. He's much more loyal to the left-wing socialist tradition of utopianism than Singer is. Singer has abandoned that sense—that "nonsense," as he puts it.

But it is because also in many ways the American Jewish and world Jewish readership is being transformed. It is renewing itself as Singer is renewing it in other writers, and it is shifting its terrain. I think that in many ways Singer is a transitional writer in that sense. A transition between the early immigrant writers that we have—American Jewish writers, Yiddish writers, and the Bellows, and Roths, and Henry Roths that will be emerging. It's kind of a figure in-between that serves as a bridge.

MORRIS DICKSTEIN: One biographical detail that should be mentioned here is that I think that he was liberated by the early death of his brother, whom he revered and whose shadow he remained in his first years when he was in America. His brother died in 1944. And I think that probably foreclosed his early attempt to be a writer like his brother, which is to say to write a multigenerational family chronicle of which we have *The Family Moskat*. And it's clear from that—though there are wonderful things in it—that his bent was not to do that kind of writing, which his brother had excelled in.

Now, curiously, his brother had always had a much more "modern" sensibility. His brother was the rebel, the one who broke away, who more clearly rejected the tradition. Whereas Bashevis Singer clearly had much more affinity for the fables, and folklore, and mysticism of his father that was in his background than his brother did. I think it was the death of his brother that not only liberated him as a writer, but helped him to become the kind of writer that he later became.

ILAN STAVANS: It's his brother who dies. Generally you have the pattern of the writer whose father is the oppressive figure—

the Kafka model. And when the father disappears, or in the case of Kafka it's a different story—the author disappears—then everything kind of falls into shape or is seen differently.

I think that sibling rivalry is very important in the case of Singer. And the fact that the brother, who has become so successful, dies on this side. It allows him to tell the story of the family in his own way.

DAVID ROSKIES: Okay, so we agree that he comes here armed with certain tools. He has the rationalist and the mystical fighting within his genes. And certain traditions that will seem exotic. But let's not forget, here was a young man, who from the age of 22 or 23 decided he was going to live from his writing, and did for the rest of his life. He was a professional writer from the word go. So, it's true, his older brother landed him a job as a proofreader in the Yiddish equivalent of *The New York Review of Books*, and he wasn't such a great proofreader. But it was a paying job. And it allowed him to enter into the literary world. He was the youngest member inducted into the Yiddish P.E.N. Club. So he was a boy wonder even in Poland. And it was in Poland, speaking about the readership—and here I'd like to sharpen this question of the American readership and what you call the transformation of that readership. What he learned to do was to differentiate his writing. He had his highbrow writing under the name Yitskhok Bashevis, and he started a little magazine with Aaron Zeitlin. And the name of that magazine was *Globus. The Globe*. You know, not anything modest! *The Globe* is what they called their little magazine in the middle of the Depression. So they were the world. And Yiddish was the world, and they were at the center of that world. So, that's where he wrote *very* tough literary criticism, that's where he serialized *Satan in Goray*.

He also wrote sensational potboilers, bordering on pornography, which he published anonymously. Although in Warsaw in literary circles everybody knew that he was one of them. He was excoriated for doing that. And then he wrote light stuff in between. So that by the time he comes to New York and he comes out of this terrible depression and writer's block, what does he do as a professional writer? He creates three literary personae, right? So he has Yitskhok Bashevis, which he always reserves for his best writing. And then he has Yitskhok Varshavski, for his middlebrow writing

79. Singer writing in his apartment in Surfside, February 12, 1986.

and his literary criticism, and for *In My Father's Court*, which he published under the middlebrow name, and all of his children's stories under the middlebrow name. And then he has a secret pen name for his tabloid journalism—D. Segal—which was only revealed, you know, very late in life.

ILAN STAVANS: He comes from the Yiddish literary tradition where using a pseudonym is a way to reinvent your persona.

MORRIS DICKSTEIN: It's also important that although he has these separate kinds of writing under different names, it's the popular writing and the desire to reach the popular audience that also undergirds the serious writing. In other words, one of the most striking things about the serious writing is its amazing concreteness. Again and again he says, writing should not be analytical. Writing should not be critical within the writing—it should be story, it should be concrete, it should be factual, it should be terse, it should be definite. And these are the kinds of things that one has to do in popular writing and immediate writing to reach an audience directly.

Now, I think the popular writing also undergirds the serious writing in a more negative way in the sense that one of the defects of some of the serious writing is this wild tendency towards melodrama. Even some of the very best stories have melodramatic twists and turns that are questionable. And I think they come from the potboilers, and they come from the more popular sensibility. So there is, I think, a series of overlaps and connections between the way he pursues each of these kinds of writing.

DAVID ROSKIES: You're absolutely right. The plot of *Satan in Goray* is: married to two men, possessed of the devil. I mean it's straight out of—

ISAIAH SHEFFER: Makes a good movie.

MAX RUDIN: It's a good headline.

DAVID ROSKIES: Yeah! That's the story! [*laughter*] It's what he does with it, though, that makes it more serious.

MAX RUDIN: What about this change from writer for a smallish Yiddish audience to writer for a mainstream English-language audience? And allied to that question, what was it that made Singer's work apposite to the American literary culture of the 50s and 60s?

MORRIS DICKSTEIN: There was a Jewish-American literary renaissance, and here was somebody who seemed to precede it, and who seemed to know so much more. Who seemed like absolutely the real article. And there were different stages in his recognition in America. The first stage, after "Gimpel the Fool" was published in *Partisan Review* and then became the title story in a very successful volume of stories, was really Singer as a sort of avant-garde writer. Not a best-selling writer—but Singer as the darling of the literary intellectuals and of the American Jewish writers and critics. Now, that was before Singer was being published in *The New Yorker*. That was when Singer was sort of a discovery of Irving Howe and the New York intellectuals.

Later, when Singer was published in *The New Yorker*, he achieved a much wider readership, just around the time that he began, after a long delay, really writing about an American setting and an American world. And so that was a different and a much wider dissemination of Singer to American readers. Then, finally, there was perhaps a third stage around the time of the Nobel Prize, where he became a monument, really. And his books were very, very widely translated abroad from the English, and he became really a world-class writer.

DAVID ROSKIES: But you're skipping the first stage, and that is the commercial failure of *The Family Moskat*. You may minimize its achievement as a modernist classic, but it is a very impressive novel. The amount of psychic energy that went into producing that novel was enormous. And the hopes that he must have had that this was going to launch his career as a Western mainstream writer, and it flopped in 1950. And it was only after the second genesis of his appearing as a cutesy storyteller that he figured out, "Ah, *that's* what they want from me."

MORRIS DICKSTEIN: But "Gimpel the Fool" was the first stage of his recognition. *The Family Moskat* was his non-recognition. In other words, it was a book that was really widely read only after the stories began to appear, and after the acclaim that he received.

ILAN STAVANS: But I go back to the issue of readership. Who gets the story published in *Partisan Review*? It starts with Eliezer Greenberg and Irving Howe. Greenberg telling Howe, "You have to read this writer." He reads it, he's mesmerized. Bellow translates it . . .

MORRIS DICKSTEIN: They stand over Bellow. Bellow is at the typewriter, and they stand over him and read him sentence by sentence. And in a couple of hours Bellow has it typed on the typewriter.

ILAN STAVANS: And so he has this cadre of people who are supporting him. *The Family Moskat* is already a failure. But a group of Jewish intellectuals, critics, writers believe that he is a link with the past that is quickly disappearing, and he begins to be championed. Without this group around him it would've been a very different story.

MORRIS DICKSTEIN: But remember this was Irving Howe more than 20 years before *World of Our Fathers*, this was Irving Howe before he became a well-known literary figure. When he was really a figure in a relatively small world of New York political and literary intellectuals. And so that was where the initial recognition came.

JONATHAN ROSEN: I think it's amazing to realize that Singer was 49 years old when this story was published. He was in some sense made by *Partisan Review*. But he was also made by the *Forward*. Irving Howe tells that story in his memoirs about discovering Singer, but he discovered Singer the way Columbus discovered America. He was there with the readership, and he had already become an incredibly accomplished writer.

And what's interesting for me to wonder about is whether even a story like "Gimpel the Fool," which suddenly was enormously appealing to American readers, had perhaps already been shaped by America, even though it was written in Yiddish. *The Family Moskat* ends, at least in English, "Death is the real Messiah"—

DAVID ROSKIES: *Only* in English.

JONATHAN ROSEN: Only in English. But that's how it was translated. But now there is a kind of element of hopefulness as well as the darkness, which may just be the reflection of his own story inside of this country.

DAVID ROSKIES: There's another aspect to his popularity in America, which is once he appears in English all of his work is radically decontextualized. Yiddish readers encountered "Gimpel the Fool" when it was written in 1945. And they read it alongside his other short stories, which complemented those told by the devil. There are actually two stories that I think were linked and he conceptualized them together. One is "Zeidlus the Pope," which is '43 or '44.

continued on page 110

Robert Giroux:

I first met Isaac Bashevis Singer when our publishing firm acquired Noonday Press. Isaac was among their authors, and when his editor, Cecil Hemley, a novelist who came with him from Noonday, left to join a university press, I succeeded as Isaac's editor. We soon became good friends, even though he was a bit shy, and at our first lunch at the Players Club on Gramercy Park, I found that he was a vegetarian and politically conservative. As I got to know Isaac better, I learned how extremely sensitive and perceptive he was, with wide-ranging interests in almost everything except modern fiction. He said the only novelists he read were dead. He was a natural wit: "I love to write for children, because they do not read book reviews. If a child likes—or fails to like—a book, nothing you say will change his or her mind. Children do not read Kafka, they like punctuation, they know that authors cannot change the world."

The first book of his I handled was *The Spinoza of Market Street*, a collection of stories. Isaac is the only author I've worked with who had a "bank" of untranslated novels and stories which had accumulated over the years in Yiddish in the *Forward*. When I met the paper's editor, Simon Weber, in Stockholm at the Nobel Prize ceremony, he told me that Isaac had not missed a single issue of the *Forward* since the mid-thirties, when he first came here from Poland. When I asked, "How is that possible?", he explained that over the years Isaac turned in dozens of full-length novels, many of which took a full year or more to publish in their weekly. "In addition, Isaac wrote many columns," he told me, "using pseudonyms, including advice to the lovelorn." Isaac was a modern writer in the Dickens tradition and his Yiddish audience was sizable. Readers wrote asking him to change details during serialization, but he said it was rarely possible, though he remembered sparing one old mother of a large family when readers begged for her survival. Isaac had lived so long in the shadow of his famous older brother that it seemed to be his lifelong literary fate. But after his brother's death and "Gimpel the Fool," when his stories began to appear in *The New Yorker*, his novels received better and better sales.

During the second year of our friendship, Isaac made a confession when I joined him for lunch at his apartment on the Upper West Side on 86th Street: "Robert, one thing I never thought would happen—I've become a rich man." This was before Hollywood had purchased "Yentl the Yeshiva Boy" or *Enemies, a Love Story*, before he had won munificent literary prizes, and when his income though steady was far from spectacular. Moved by his comment, I could only say, "Isaac, you ain't seen nothin' yet." Many years later, after the Nobel Prize, movie sales, and best-seller royalties, I had a phone call from the Superintendent of West Point, who asked me to persuade Isaac to lecture at the military academy to the cadets on the subject of freedom for one hour. It was an endowed series and the fee was ten thousand dollars, an offer I thought he could not refuse, but to my surprise he said no. When I asked him why, he said he had two reasons: "One, I don't know any generals and two, 'freedom' is much too abstract a subject. I wouldn't know what to say." I urged him for several days to reconsider and suggested as a topic the freedom of the writer. He finally agreed, provided I would join him and a group of friends at West Point. On the appointed day we had a full-dress review of the entire cadet corps at sunset, when they marched by on the open field in white-trousered precision. As they did so, I heard Isaac whisper, "Some of these men are women. I saw four or five." The Superintendent told us that Isaac was the hit of the series. He made the cadets laugh, especially during the post-lecture question period, when a young cadet piped up with some query and Isaac asked, "Was that a man or a woman?" and the cadets howled with glee. "It's hard to tell anymore," Isaac added.

He always wrote in Yiddish, on a typewriter whose ancient carriage moved from the right. His English became so good that he decided to do his own translations, most of the time with assistants, usually with women. Dorothea Straus, who worked with him on his fiction, especially his *New Yorker* stories, told me that she knew no Yiddish. They sat together and he translated orally, sentence by sentence. Her suggestions were mainly minor, to clarify or to simplify, and she said he got better and better. He was popular abroad and the foreign editions of his work were almost always based on the English versions. When we met, his written English was quite good, though his pronunciation was less so. By the time he asked me to accompany him to Stockholm for the Nobel Prize ceremony, his mastery of English was nearly perfect. In his witty address to the Swedish Academy, he read one sentence in Yiddish, and when the official came and told us it had been a historic occasion, I thought he was referring to this until he said, "No, it's the first time to my knowledge that the Swedish Academy has ever laughed."

Isaac had an impressive knowledge of Jewish traditions and lore, which is obvious from all his books. In his novel *The Certificate* there is a portrait of an old rabbi, the father of the hero who is trying to leave Poland, which I am certain is based on his father because it is written with love and respect. Yet Isaac said he and his brother disappointed their father by joining modern movements of "enlightenment." The mother of Isaac's son was a dedicated communist, who took their child to the Soviet Union, where she was soon expelled and escaped to Palestine in the late thirties, where they joined a kibbutz. I met the son, Israel Zamir, on the night of the royal banquet in Stockholm when he knocked on my door at the hotel, holding a camera and wearing white tie and tails, like all the guests. He wanted me to take his picture, "since no one at the kibbutz will believe how I'm dressed unless I can show them a photo," and of course I did so.

After Isaac's death in 1991, we continued to publish works kept in the *Forward*'s "bank," books like *Meshugah*,

The King of the Fields, and *Scum.* But it was *Shadows on the Hudson,* written in the 1950s, that received the highest praise. Richard Bernstein called it "a piercing work of fiction with a strong claim to being Singer's masterpiece." Bernstein followed with an unprecedented second daily rave, after the reviewer in the Sunday book section of the *Times* gave it its only bad review. Ron Rosenbaum also wrote a two-part review, calling it a "passionate, perfectly crafted work. Nowhere is Singer's power, that chastening blackness of his vision, stronger or more penetrating."

Alma Singer, Isaac's widow, invited me to attend the blessing of his tombstone at a New Jersey cemetery. I noticed on arrival that the engraver had misspelled "*Noble* Prize" on the headstone. After the blessing, when the rabbi asked me as Isaac's editor to say a few words, I managed to justify the mistake (which was later corrected) by praising the "extraordinary, even noble, literary career of Isaac Bashevis Singer."

81. Singer's tombstone in the Beth-El Cemetery in Paramus, New Jersey, with "Noble Laureate" now corrected to read "Nobel Laureate."

And the other is "Gimpel the Fool." They're the same story, two aspects of it. One is a person who is destroyed because he is all mind and rationalism. Taken to an absolute extreme. The boy wonder who then wants to become a pope and is undone by his hubris.

JONATHAN ROSEN: And he sells out to Christian culture.

DAVID ROSKIES: Yes. Right, then he sells out. But is redeemed in the penultimate moment of his life when he says, "If you, the devil, are real, then God is real." So he has that transcendental moment, which is given to him despite everything that he fought for and labored over. And then you have Gimpel, the man of perfect faith, who achieves transcendence through the school of hard knocks, and being cuckolded once, and then again, and being the butt of everybody's joke.

I think that is a rewriting, a modernist revision of one of the classic Hasidic stories of Nachman of Bratslav, the story of the wise man and the fool. So you have the two characters, the wise man and the fool. Only he splits them and creates two characters.

But the important thing, the point is this: He writes them in the very midst of the Holocaust. The end of that civilization. And it is his response to the two—these are two different but complementary responses to the Holocaust. By the time these works appear in English one is in *Partisan Review* in 1953. "Zeidlus" appears in 1960 in a random collection—you know, the third collection of short stories, in the middle of all this other stuff. So, whatever he was trying to say at that particular moment to that particular audience is lost.

MORRIS DICKSTEIN: But remember, "Gimpel" is the rewriting of the greatest Yiddish *shlemiel* story, I. L. Peretz's "Bontsha Schweig" ("Bontsha the Silent"). And I think the idea of the fool, who through his simplicity achieves a kind of transcendence, is possibly the most traditional motif that Singer ever used.

ILAN STAVANS: But if you take it out of Yiddish literature and again see it from the other side, "Gimpel the Fool" is an astonishing rewriting of *Don Quixote*. I was just rereading the new translation, and you see a fool just going from one episode to another, everybody takes advantage of him, and in the end he wins.

MORRIS DICKSTEIN: Maybe that's the definition of a classic. It's the rewriting of everything.

ISAIAH SHEFFER: There was also that elfin interview persona that he developed. He is said to have answered to the question, "How come 'Gimpel' was such a success?"—"Perhaps people thought it was about Gimbel's. I think I'll call my next book Macy's. . . ." [*laughter*] I wouldn't vouch for that quote.

ILAN STAVANS: But it's a good one.

MORRIS DICKSTEIN: I wouldn't vouch for the following story that I heard on good authority. Singer was invited to speak at the University of Texas, and there was going to be a huge audience. And a young man was sent to accompany him, he met him at the airport. He was trying to be very helpful, and he said, "Mr. Singer, I'll be there. After your reading there'll be a question period. Is there any particular question that you would like to speak about? I could ask it from the audience." And he said, "You know, a lot of people have compared my work to that of Marc Chagall. Perhaps you would ask me what I would think about a comparison of my work to Marc Chagall."

And so the event occurs and there's the question period and the discussion. The young man in the back raises his hand and says, "Mr. Singer, I wonder how would you compare your work to that of Marc Chagall?" And he says, "Now that is the stupidest question I have ever heard."

DAVID ROSKIES: Except that it really happened to the head of the English Department. It wasn't just a hapless undergrad. [*laughter*]

MORRIS DICKSTEIN: Well, these stories change in the retelling.

MAX RUDIN: I'd like to ask, what does it mean to have Singer in The Library of America? Does Singer's work in any way expand our idea of what the possibilities of American literature are?

JONATHAN ROSEN: I think Singer became an American writer for lots of reasons. One of them is that immigrant writers in general dramatized an aspect of the American experience so that people on the periphery suddenly seemed to be at the center of the dramatic story. But I also think that there is a strain in America itself that was compatible to Singer. And I don't know if he willed it into being, or if it happened just because he was living in this country. You think about a novel like *The Slave*, which is set in the seventeenth century, and the detail and the evocation of Poland in the seventeenth century is incredibly rich. But there's something about the love story that is so contemporary. And the hero of that story is a kind of American solitary figure. There's an Emersonian sense, almost, of self-reliance in that book that is very much at odds with traditional Eastern European notions of Jewish community. And it's a very natural transformation. I don't know if it was done consciously. But you simply feel it in that book. It feels like an American book. There's an element of American consciousness in it. And although it has the trappings of Jewishness in it, it really feels more like a kind of American religion, where the journey is inward, and the salvation of the self is the individual's salvation. There's a powerful strain of individualism in Singer that he discovers in himself, I think, that just fits in an American tradition.

Also, the flip side of that is the sense of America as a place of—a sense of chosenness gone wrong. I think the greatest novel in the nineteenth century in America is *Moby-Dick*, about a whole community—a whale ship—that sinks, and everybody's destroyed except for one guy with a Biblical name who tells the story. And there's a way in which that solitary narrator riding the aftermath of calamity is very much in tune with what Singer is doing. I don't think he's doing it consciously, but I think there was something in the air, or something in the atmosphere, and something perhaps about America itself, having been born out of certain Jewish ideas as transformed by Protestantism that you hear an echo of in some sense in his writing.

DAVID ROSKIES: That's very funny—or it's wonderful, because I was told that the other country where he is most popular is Italy, because all his readers are lapsed Catholics. And they identify with the drama that gets played out with all these penitents and all these rebels, all these fornicators who really want to go back and pray and be cleansed of their sins. So, you're right—I think there's a religious dimension to his writing which is remarkably modern.

MORRIS DICKSTEIN: And there's the sexual dimension, which is to say that Singer was early on seen as unusually modern in his treatment of sex, and passion, and love. And he was seen as different from other Yiddish writers, less traditional than other Yiddish writers for that reason. And I think that relates to the individualism that we might feel in Singer's work, as compared to the communalism. He had a kind of fatalism, and he felt that human beings are like puppets who play out their little dramas on earth for a very short period. He had a vision of life that promoted the idea that we should live all we can and live out our desires, even though it may lead us to be kind of shadows who are just dancing around in a void. Both a gloomy, grim, dark philosophy at the same time—one that had to do with a very positive view of living in the moment, and particularly about living sexually.

MAX RUDIN: Let's pick up two phrases. One is your "shadows dancing in the void," and the other is Jonathan's reference to *Moby-Dick*: "And I alone have escaped to tell thee." Let's talk about the Holocaust and Singer's work. Does the Holocaust change the meaning and direction of Singer's work?

ILAN STAVANS: The Holocaust has become such a cathartic, such a cataclysmic event in Jewish history, in world history, that you can't write the same, you can't think the same, and you don't have the same audience. So I think it's simply that the zeitgeist has been transformed, and the void is there, and you'll respond to that void.

JONATHAN ROSEN: I think you can answer the question of the effect of the Holocaust on Singer in a hundred ways and a hundred times. It was just so profound. But I think it's amazing to realize how cold his eye had to be to be able to write with such energy—to almost be liberated by the Holocaust.

I remember when I was at the *Forward*, the old Yiddishists would sort of talk about Singer's brother as if he was not only a better writer, but that he kind of had the tact and integrity to die in 1944 when everybody else was dying. Whereas Bashevis Singer was suddenly energized and had this whole other career, in which he was also free to reinvent what was gone and shape it around his own imagination. So it's half tribute, but it's half transformation.

DAVID ROSKIES: It's not, almost. We have the documents to prove it. He writes an essay in 1943, "Concerning Yiddish Writing in Poland." The most anti-sentimental overview of Yiddish culture. It's written in the Holocaust issue of *Di zukunft*, which was the leading Yiddish periodical. It was the first time that all the surviving writers were asked to respond.

82. Singer in the Garden Cafeteria, Lower East Side, 1982.

They all do by writing jeremiads. It's August 1943, Yiddish writers—if nobody else in this world—knew exactly what had happened. Polish Jewry was over, was finished. And he writes this scathing, scathing review of Yiddish between the two world wars, where he says that it was *getlekh on a got, veltlekh on a velt*: "It was godly without believing in God. It was worldly without having a world to stand on." That's it.

So I think just as you said before, the death of his brother in 1944 and the death of Eastern Europe was absolutely liberating in terms of allowing him to reinvent the past. But I would also say that's sort of a misanthropic, maybe, side of it. The other thing is something you said when we talked about *Shadows on the Hudson*. Let's not forget that from the get-go, he identified Nazism and communism as two equal evil empires. And you can see that in "The Cafeteria," you can see that in *Shadows on the Hudson*, you can see that in *Enemies*—in all these stories where the Holocaust is invoked—for him, those who survived the gulag are functionally the same as those who survived the death camps.

MORRIS DICKSTEIN: Remember, Singer very clearly—if we can identify him at all with the survivor characters in *Enemies* or in *Shadows on the Hudson*—felt a great deal of survivor guilt. It's true that the Holocaust, by finishing off the older Yiddish culture, had in a sense liberated him. And yet I think he felt—and his characters all feel—his characters are like the survivor characters in *Shadows on the Hudson*. They are like the living dead. They are shadows, they are unreal. They feel that they're living a weightless, unreal life.

Although Singer adapted to America very well, his characters universally detest many features of American life and find them thin, and materialistic, and culturally insubstantial compared to Europe. I think one of the things that makes for Singer's greatness is this ambivalence—these many threads of feeling that include very negative feelings about America—that he has from the very beginning.

JONATHAN ROSEN: If the Holocaust hadn't happened—one of course can't imagine it—the writers who elevated him in *Partisan Review* would have been much more wary of him. He would have been the return of the repressed—the thing that they were separating themselves from. But there was an almost automatic sentimentalization and an awareness of what was gone. And so there was a need for people to fill it.

MORRIS DICKSTEIN: Remember, these writers had by and large until that point not at all identified themselves with their Jewishness. In fact, they had done everything they could, including in most cases changing their names, to separate themselves from their Jewishness. Secretly they found that they were all really very Jewish. But Singer appeared on the scene at just the moment when they were sort of rediscovering their Jewishness, partly because of the war, partly because their politics had changed. And he gave them a version of the past—not that they had rejected, but that they almost knew nothing about—that was unsentimental, hard and sharp. That was brilliant and bitter. This was a version that they could accept much more than they could in any writer that would have sentimentalized them.

MAX RUDIN: Do you think Singer was lucky in his timing in the sense that the 60s and 70s was a time when a kind of American Jewish culture itself was moving from periphery to mainstream? People started to eat bagels and cream cheese, and suddenly things which had been ethnic were now pop culture. Is there any connection there, or is that simply factitious?

MORRIS DICKSTEIN: Well, Singer never became popular in that way. He was never exported to every foreign city like a bagel. So, I wonder. I think there was a period when Jews and Jewish culture became culturally fashionable, and he both profited from that and his work indeed helped to fuel that.

Just two weeks ago I was at a conference on immigrant literature at this Key West seminar and immigrant literature most definitely did not include the Jews. The one Russian Jewish writer who was supposed to be there didn't come. The one Eastern European Jewish writer there clearly felt more Eastern European than she felt Jewish. Clearly, the dynamic element that was there in terms of present-day immigrant writers were Hispanic writers and Asian-American writers. So, in a way things have moved on.

But they've moved on in a way that tells us what it was like for Jewish writers in the 40s, and 50s and 60s, especially if you factor in a huge amount of guilt about the Holocaust. In other words, America was not responsible for the Holocaust, but America certainly didn't do enough to try to prevent it or to intervene. And therefore you see the effect on American mores. Discrimination, anti-Semitism in America was a very, very common feature of American life before World War II. And for 25 to 30 years after the war it almost disappeared because of this guilt element about the Holocaust. Whether that worked in favor of Jewish writers as well, I'm not sure. Certainly some popular books by Jewish writers like, let's say, *Exodus* or something like that fit into kind of an American pop sensibility the way Saul Bellow and I. B. Singer never could.

DAVID ROSKIES: I think the secret of his success was that he made absolutely no demands of his readers. Singer never took a classic work of Yiddish literature to translate it and said, you know, "If you really want to learn Yiddish this is why you should learn Yiddish. And I will show you that there is a great tradition out there." Or not Yiddish. Take some other: there are other Jewish classics that he could've turned to. He didn't mentor any younger writers. He was always very competitive toward anybody else.

And in the process of translation he dumbed himself down. He knew what he was doing in terms of what the expectation of the readers was going to be. I think that was also a brilliant calculation on his part so that he could become the Jewish writer for all seasons in a culture that was basically middlebrow.

MORRIS DICKSTEIN: But when he very belatedly begins writing about survivors and Jews in America, long, long after he's lived here, he really does open up a new vein in his work, and really in a different style. That's a very striking development. He doesn't keep mining the demonic modernist—the dybbuk style—into the 70s and 80s. Absolutely not. And he was also, remember, tremendously productive into his old age. And these late stories, like "The Cafeteria" are not like "Gimpel the Fool."

JONATHAN ROSEN: That's a good story.

DAVID ROSKIES: It's not that late—'68.

MORRIS DICKSTEIN: Well, that's pretty late. How old was he? In his mid-60s.

ILAN STAVANS: The Singer we remember in photographs is the old Singer, the one that has lost his hair, the one that is making jokes, being impatient, being antsy. And it's a kind of grandfatherly figure. I think it is important to just bring here the fact that he had a very conflicted relationship with his son. That descendency, as we were saying, within the literary tradition is very problematic. That he doesn't cater and push anybody new to the fore, and yet he becomes this kind of sage for American Jews and for American culture.

JONATHAN ROSEN: And a children's book writer.

DAVID ROSKIES: *Naftali the Storyteller and His Horse, Sus* is the rewriting of "Gimpel the Fool," where he portrays himself in a much more benign light as a grandfatherly, sage storyteller.

MORRIS DICKSTEIN: It happened that as an old man—and even as a slightly younger man—he fit very well into an American literary culture that was much more about authors as characters and personalities than it was about books. He had already crafted this persona that fit very well into what became of American literary culture in the 60s and 70s, which was to a degree a celebrity culture. And he became a fixture in that celebrity culture.

JONATHAN ROSEN: And simultaneously an avocation of a standard figure in Yiddish literature, like Mendele. He was just a guy going around telling stories.

DAVID ROSKIES: And feeding the pigeons.

83. Singer feeding pigeons on Broadway.

Jerome Rothenberg: It was through Singer that I first saw an opening to what came to be, for a number of years at least, a center of my work. I met him only once, in 1957, a year or so after the American publication of *Satan in Goray*, and it took me at least a decade to absorb that book and the books that followed into my own system of writing and thinking. Our meeting was arranged by Cecil Hemley, who was Singer's editor at Noonday Press, with the mistaken idea that I might know enough Yiddish to take on some of the translation for what was coming to be a major Noonday project. Singer was only just getting to be known—outside of Yiddish circles anyway—but my own reading of *Satan in Goray* and the *Gimpel the Fool* stories was already working on my imagination with a sense of something new that might find a way into the poetry I was then learning to compose.

84. Singer photographed through the window of a New York City restaurant.

Two things stand out in my memory. The first was Singer's reaction to a recent review in the *Times*—Irving

Howe writing on *Satan* or on *Gimpel*, or possibly on both. Hemley brought this up over lunch, in particular a comment by Howe that Singer was a "cruel" writer, and asked him what he thought about that. Singer shrugged it off with a comment that stuck with me and that I often repeated: "Since when has cruelty been a crime?" (Or maybe he said "a sin"; I've told it differently at different times.) I was still a young poet at the time, and a statement like that had a real *frisson* for me.

The other thing I remember was that I asked him whether there were any Yiddish poets who did anything comparable to what he was doing in his fictions. We talked about what that comparable thing, that quality, might be, and in the end he came up with a blank and an indication, I thought, that the matter was of no great concern to him. It was to me, however, and it began to confront me with a question to which I still had no answer—if there were such a Yiddish poetry, a poetry of *cruelty* in Artaud's sense (or Singer's for that matter), what form would that poetry take?

In 1967, as I was completing work on my book *Technicians of the Sacred* and mapping tribal and oral poetries on a global scale, I decided to explore "ancestral sources of my own in a world of Jewish mystics, thieves, & madmen." The initial thrust came from a concurrent reading of Singer and Gertrude Stein—two very different artists but both of them crucial for what I meant to undertake. In a 12-part poem of Stein's called "Dates," I came across what I took to be Stein's "Jewish poem"—the words "pass" and "over" repeated a number of times: "Pass over / Pass over / Pass / Pass / Pass / Pass / Pass pass," to which I added a final line: "Pass water." I then went over the other parts of her poem, referring constantly to *Satan in Goray* and substituting words of Singer's for words of Stein's while retaining her pattern of syllables and rhymings. Thus, where Stein's first numbered section read "Fish. / Bequeath fish. / Able to state papers. / Fish. / Bequeath fish," mine read "Sect. / Avert sect. / Avert to wash bellies. / Sect. / Avert sect." I called the resultant poem "Satan in Goray" and subtitled it "A Homage to Isaac Bashevis Singer."

For me the work that followed was a book-length poem or poem-series called *Poland/1931*. While most of the poems in *Poland* departed sharply from the opening Stein imitation, Singer's books remained part of the body of largely documentary materials from which I drew toward the construction of an imagined (I stress *imagined*) Jewish Poland. That work was my own attempt at a fiction of some dimension or what fellow poet Edward Sanders included in another context as an "investigative poetry" made up of "radiant data clusters." For this, Singer was one of my guides into that Jewish underworld toward which my poetry was tentatively reaching.

Such an underworld—and its sexual side in particular—was a block, I later found, for many of Singer's Yiddish readers. In my own family, Singer's brother and other Yiddish novelists were cited as his superiors, for reasons that I felt and still feel were spurious. But for other readers of his Yiddish and for those of us who were reading him in English, his work was an incitement and a path to those "Jewish mysteries that one confronts in a place no less dangerous or real than that abyss of the Aztecs: . . . *a difficult, a dangerous place, a deathly place: it is dark, it is light.* . . ." Or so I wrote in the preface to *A Big Jewish Book* (a.k.a. *Exiled in the Word*), my revisionist anthology of Jewish poetry "from tribal times to the present." Of course I included Singer in that one among the many "cruel poets" (old and new) for whom he was, I thought, an always present, always necessary, ally.

Contributors

Nicholas Dawidoff is the author of *The Fly Swatter* (2002), *In the Country of Country* (1997), and *The Catcher Was a Spy* (1994). He edited the Library of America collection *Baseball: A Literary Anthology* (2002).

Morris Dickstein is Distinguished Professor of English at Queens College and the Graduate Center of the City University of New York. He is the author of *Leopards in the Temple: The Transformation of American Fiction 1945–1970* (2002).

Jonathan Safran Foer is the author of the novel *Everything Is Illuminated* (2002).

James Gibbons is Associate Editor at The Library of America.

Robert Giroux is a partner of the publishing house Farrar, Straus & Giroux.

Joyce Carol Oates is a novelist and short-story writer whose many books include *Rape: A Love Story* (2003), *Beasts* (2002), and *We Were the Mulvaneys* (1996).

Cynthia Ozick is a fiction writer and essayist whose books include *Quarrel and Quandary* (2000) and *The Puttermesser Papers* (1997).

Francine Prose is the author of *The Lives of the Muses: Nine Women and the Artists They Inspired* (2002), as well many works of fiction including *Blue Angel* (2000) and *Guided Tours of Hell* (1997).

Jonathan Rosen is the author of *The Talmud and the Internet* (2000) and the novel *Eve's Apple* (1997).

David Roskies is Professor of Jewish Literature at the Jewish Theological Seminary of America. He is the author of *A Bridge of Longing: The Lost Art of Yiddish Storytelling* (1995) and *Against the Apocalypse* (1984). He is a founding co-editor of *Prooftexts: A Journal of Jewish Literary History*.

Jerome Rothenberg is a poet and anthologist whose books include the two-volume anthology *Poems for the Millenium* (with Pierre Joris, 1995–1998), *Technicians of the Sacred* (1985), and *Revolution of the Word* (1974). He is Professor of Visual Arts and Literature at the University of California, San Diego.

Max Rudin is Publisher of The Library of America.

Harvey Shapiro is a poet whose books include *How Charlie Shavers Died and Other Poems* (2001) and *Selected Poems* (1997). He edited the Library of America anthology *Poets of World War II* in 2003. He was editor of *The New York Times Book Review* from 1975 to 1983 and for many years was an editor at *The New York Times Magazine*.

Isaiah Sheffer is Artistic Director of Symphony Space in New York City and the host of National Public Radio's "Selected Shorts."

Ilan Stavans, editor, is Lewis-Sebring Professor in Latin American and Latino Culture at Amherst College. He is the editor of The Library of America's three-volume edition of Isaac Bashevis Singer's *Collected Stories*, published in 2004. He is the author of *Spanglish: The Making of a New American Language* (2003).

Sources

8 "If you . . . country": Grace Farrell (ed.), *Conversations* (Jackson: University of Mississippi Press, 1992), p. 51.

9 "My grandfather . . . time": *In My Father's Court* (New York: Farrar, Straus & Giroux), p. 287. "In this world . . . history": *In My Father's Court*, p. 290. "In the wintertime . . ."; "We were refugees . . .": Typescript, Harry Ransom Center for the Humanities, University of Texas at Austin.

11 "Processes . . . rain": "Concerning Yiddish Literature in Poland (1943)," translated by Robert Wolf: *Prooftexts* 15:2 (1995), pp. 113–114. (*caption*) "Amid . . . cemetery": *Collected Stories: Gimpel the Fool to The Letter Writer* (New York: The Library of America, 2004), p. 20. Hereafter cited as LOA I. (*caption*) "He . . . pious": *In My Father's Court*, p. 46.

12 "blend of a court . . . themselves": *In My Father's Court*, p. vii. "salacious . . . thoughts": *Love and Exile: An Autobiographical Trilogy* (New York: Doubleday, 1984), p. xvi. "we were never . . . regulations": *In My Father's Court*, p. 68.

13 (*caption*) "There were some . . . gifts": *In My Father's Court*, p. 162.

15 "Hasid in skirts"; "mild attacks of epilepsy"; "seemed possessed by a dibbuk": *In My Father's Court*, p. 151. "struck . . . escape": Zalman Shneour, *Downfall* (New York: Roy Publishers, 1944), p. 9. "Mother and I . . . calamities": *Shosha*, translated by Joseph Singer and Isaac Bashevis Singer (New York: Farrar, Straus & Giroux, 1978), p. 13.

17 "half-bog, half-village": *Love and Exile*, p. 42. "Here I saw . . . nations": Israel Joshua Singer, *Nay Rusland* (*New Russia*, 1928), quoted and translated in Henrietta Mondry and Joseph Sherman, "Russian Dogs and Jewish Russians: Reading Israel Joshua Singer's "Liuk" in a Russian Literary Context": *Prooftexts* 20:3 (2000), p. 314.

19 "bourse . . . Poland": "Concerning Yiddish Literature in Poland," p. 122. New arrivals . . . Yiddish: "Concerning Yiddish Literature in Poland," p. 123.

21 (*caption*) "When Esther . . . goyish": *Love and Exile*, p. 211.

22 "town . . . world"; "They slaughtered . . . slavery": *Satan in Goray*, translated by Jacob Sloan (New York: The Noonday Press, 1955), pp. 3–4.

23 "living . . . repute": *Satan in Goray*, p. 34. "beset by mysterious ills": *Satan in Goray*, p. 68. "reckoned . . . day": *Satan in Goray*, p. 6. "In this work . . . activism": *Satan in Goray*, p. x.

26 (*caption*) "I have . . . work": Kenneth Turan, "Isaac Bashevis Singer: 'I Walk on Mysteries,'" *Washington Post*, December 28, 1976, p. C1.

29 (*caption*) "She was . . . poetry"; "From morning . . . writers": "When the Old World Came to Sea Gate," *New York Times*, January 2, 1972, p. A2.

34 "Nearly everyone . . . paper"; "Some . . . true it was": *Love and Exile*, p. 271.

35 "wilderness": *Collected Stories: A Friend of Kafka to Passions* (New York: The Library of America, 2004), p. 637. Hereafter cited as LOA II.

37 "There was no moon . . . achieve": LOA II, p. 647. "young, slim . . . good book": quoted in Janet Hadda, *Isaac Bashevis Singer: A Biography* (New York: Oxford University Press, 1997), p. 96.

42 "since it was . . . former size": LOA I, p. 328.

43 Then the building . . . hoarsely: LOA I, p. 154.

44 "godly . . . world": "Concerning Yiddish Literature in Poland," p. 120. "His characters . . . memories": "Concerning Yiddish Literature in Poland," p. 127. "Long before . . . work": "Concerning Yiddish Literature in Poland," p. 120.

45 "Neologisms . . . do so": "Problems of Yiddish Prose in America (1943)," translated by Robert Wolf. *Prooftexts* 9:1 (1989), p. 9.

46 "master": Acknowledgments page of *The Family Moskat*, translated by A. H. Gross (New York, Knopf, 1950); LOA I, p. 332; *Love and Exile*, p. 258.

47 "All Frampol . . . stock in": LOA I, p. 13.

48 "I agree heartily . . . cut": Letter from Alfred Knopf to Singer dated August 25, 1949, Harry Ransom Center, University of Texas at Austin. **"Death . . . truth"**: *The Family Moskat*, p. 611. **"Yours . . . Messiah"**: "*The Family Moskat*: Chapter 65," translated by Joseph C. Landis, *Yiddish*, Summer–Fall 1985, p. 116. **"titles of interest"; "throbbing vitality"**: "Nine Titles of Interest in the Field of Current Fiction," *The New York Times Book Review*, October 22, 1950, p. 18.

52 "in a state of high enchantment": Irving Howe, *A Margin of Hope* (New York: Harcourt Brace Jovanovich, 1982), p. 262. **"I had seven . . . fool"**: LOA I, p 5. **"that was no go either"**: LOA I, p. 6. **"How often . . . new writer?"**: Howe, *A Margin of Hope*, p. 262.

53 "Deeply learned . . . skepticism": Irving Howe and Eliezer Greenberg (eds.), *A Treasury of Yiddish Stories* (New York: The Viking Press, 1954), p 86.

56 "began . . . friendship": Israel Zamir, *Journey to My Father, Isaac Bashevis Singer*, translated by Barbara Harshav (New York: Arcade Publishing, 1995), p. vii. (*caption*) **"He had sent . . . phantom"**: LOA II, p. 209.

57 "an autobiography I never intend to write": *Love and Exile*, p. vii.

58 Once again . . . all this last?: *Shadows on the Hudson*, translated by Joseph Sherman (New York, Farrar, Straus & Giroux, 1998), p. 90. Hereafter cited as *Shadows*. **The wider America . . . crisis**: *Shadows*, p. 198.

61 (*caption*) **"Singer . . . anywhere"**: quoted in Paul Kresh, *Isaac Bashevis Singer: The Magician of West 86th Street* (New York: The Dial Press, 1979), p. 191.

66 "mired in his own originality": Irving Howe (ed.), *Selected Short Stories of Isaac Bashevis Singer* (New York: The Modern Library, 1966), p. xxi. **"Singer seems . . . stasis"**: Irving Howe, "Stories: New, Old, and Sometimes Good," *The New Republic*, November 13, 1961, pp. 22–23.

67 "I dictate them . . . English": Morton A. Reichek, "Storyteller," *The New York Times Magazine*, March 23, 1975, pp. 21. **"second original language"**: LOA II, p. 271.

70 "I write . . . another": Turan, "Isaac Bashevis Singer: 'I Walk on Mysteries,'" p. C3.

71 "father and mother . . . Singer": quoted in *The Art of Maurice Sendak, Volume 2: 1980 to the Present. Essay by Tony Kushner* (New York: Harry N. Abrams, 2003), p. 35.

72 "like an animal . . . shoot": *Collected Stories: One Night in Brazil to The Death of Methuselah* (New York: The Library of America, 2004), p. 110. **"an escape-artist, the sex-Houdini"; "cherished mistress"**: quoted in Kresh, *Isaac Bashevis Singer*, pp. 126–127. **"agreed hatred . . . stories"** and subsequent quotes on pp. *72–73*: Cynthia Ozick, "Envy; or, Yiddish in America" in *The Pagan Rabbi* (New York: Knopf, 1971), pp. 46–48.

75 "No writer . . . suicide": *The New York Times Book Review*, November 9, 1969, A1. **"One of modern man's . . . theories"**: *The Penitent* (New York: Farrar, Straus & Giroux, 1983), p. 160.

76 "The agonies . . . recognized": *The Penitent*, p. 170.

82 "children read books, not reviews"; "and nothing . . . language": www.nobel.se/literature/laureates/1978/singer-speech.html. **"entertainer of the spirit"** and other quotes from Singer's Nobel Lecture on Literature: www.nobel.se/literature/laureates/1978/singer-lecture.html.

83 "has vitamins . . . got": Elenore Lester, "At 71, Isaac Bashevis Singer Makes His Broadway Debut." *The New York Times*, April 26, 1975. See also Reichek, "Storyteller," p. 16.

85 "a hub of Jewishness"; "a continuation of the little town"; "saw again . . . home"; "The sound . . . as ever": *My Love Affair with Miami Beach: Photographs by Richard Nagler with introduction and commentary by Isaac Bashevis Singer* (New York: Simon & Schuster, 1991), p. vii. **"stronghold . . . soul"**: *In My Father's Court*, p. 68. **"here . . . religion"**: *Shadows*, p. 146. **"Mankind . . . animals"**: LOA I, p. 372. **"People lose their minds in America"**: LOA II, p. 597.

86 "I must say . . . absent"; "This kitsch ending . . . commercial value": "I. B. Singer Talks to I. B. Singer about the Movie *Yentl*," *The New York Times*, January 29, 1984, p. H1.

87 "He was just . . . his writing": quoted in Hadda, *Isaac Bashevis Singer: A Biography*, p. 213.

Photo Credits

The Library of America extends its special thanks to the Harry Ransom Humanities Research Center, to researcher Eric Lupfer, and to photographer Abe Frajndlich for his generosity.

Great care has been taken to locate and acknowledge all owners of copyrighted material in this book. If any such owner has inadvertently been omitted, acknowledgment will gladly be made in future printings.

Harry Ransom Humanities Research Center, The University of Texas at Austin. Reprinted by permission.
> Frontispiece, 6, 9, 12, 13, 14, 15, 18, 19, 20, 21, 22, 25, 30, 31, 32, 33, 34, 35, 36, 38, 50, 51, 52, 53, 54, 56, 57, 63, 65, 66, 67, 72, 73, 77, 78, 80, 84

Laura Ziegler © 1971. Reprinted by permission of the artist. All rights reserved.
> 1

Antonio Frasconi © 1983. Reprinted by permission of the artist. All rights reserved.
> 2

A. Trzcinski. Reprinted by permission of the photographer.
> 3

Farrar, Straus & Giroux, Inc. Reprinted from *A Day of Pleasure and Other Stories for Children* © 1991. By permisson of the publisher.
> 4, 5, 11

Reprinted by permission of the publisher.
> 46, 47, 48

Archives of the YIVO Institute for Jewish Research. Reprinted by permission.
> 7, 16, 17, 23, 42 (portrait of I. J. Singer)

International Center of Photography. © Mara Vishniac Kohn. Reprinted by permission.
> 8, 10

Forward Association Photo Archive. Reprinted by permission. All rights reserved.
> 24, 39, 40

Florida Atlantic University Libraries, Boca Raton, Florida. Reprinted by permission.
> 26, 37

Museum of the City of New York. © Berenice Abbott. Reprinted by permission.
> 27, 28

Random House, Inc. Reprinted by permission.
> 29, 43, 44, 45

The New York Times. © 1944. Reprinted by permission.
> 41 (obituary)

Paul Giovanopoulos. © 1967. Reprinted by permission of the artist. All rights reserved.
> 49

Condé Nast, Inc. Reprinted by permission.
> 55

Iris Schneider. © Iris Schneider. Reprinted by permission of the photographer. All rights reserved.
> 58

HarperCollins, Inc. Reprinted by permission.
> 59

Abe Frajndlich. © Abe Frajndlich. Reprinted by permission of the photographer. All rights reserved.
> 60, 69, 70, 75, 76, 79, 85, last page (Singer in his Manhattan apartment, February 12, 1986)

85. Singer and Alma.